Theoretical Aspects
of
Aging

ACADEMIC PRESS RAPID MANUSCRIPT REPRODUCTION

Proceedings of a Symposium on the
Theoretical Aspects of Aging
Held in Miami, Florida
February 7-8, 1974

Theoretical Aspects
of
Aging

Edited by

Morris Rockstein

Associate Editor
Marvin L. Sussman

Assistant Editor
Jeffrey Chesky

Department of Physiology and Biophysics
University of Miami School of Medicine
Miami, Florida

ACADEMIC PRESS, INC.   New York   San Francisco   London   1974
A Subsidiary of Harcourt Brace Jovanovich, Publishers

599.0372
Sy 6t
92489
Mar. 1975

ACADEMIC PRESS, INC.
111 Fifth Avenue, New York, New York 10003

United Kingdom Edition published by
ACADEMIC PRESS, INC. (LONDON) LTD.
24/28 Oval Road, London NW1

Library of Congress Cataloging in Publication Data

Symposium on the Theoretical Aspects of Aging, Miami,
    Fla., 1974.
    Theoretical aspects of aging.

    Bibliography: p.
    1. Aging–Congresses.   I.   Rockstein, Morris,
ed.   II.   Title.   [DNLM: 1.   Aging–Congresses.
WT104 T396]
QP86.S9 1974   599'.03'72   74-12451
ISBN 0–12–591655–8

CONTENTS

CONTENTS

CONTRIBUTORS

William H. Adler, Laboratory of Cellular and Comparative Physiology, Gerontology Research Center, Baltimore City Hospitals, Baltimore, Maryland 21224

Reubin Andres, Clinical Physiology Branch, Gerontology Research Center, Baltimore City Hospitals, Baltimore, Maryland 21224

Ana Aslan, The Bucharest Institute of Geriatrics, Bucharest, Romania

Johan Bjorksten, Bjorksten Research Foundation, Madison, Wisconsin 53701

Seymour Gelfant, Departments of Dermatology and Cell and Molecular Biology, Medical College of Georgia, Augusta, Georgia 30902

Paul Gordon, Department of Physiology, Northwestern University School of Medicine, Chicago, Illinois 60680

Gary L. Grove, Department of Dermatology, Medical College of Georgia, Augusta, Georgia, 30902

Leonard Hayflick, Department of Medical Microbiology, Stanford University School of Medicine, Stanford, California 94305

J. Earle Officer, Department of Pathology, University of Southern California School of Medicine, Los Angeles, California 90033

Morris Rockstein, Department of Physiology and Biophysics, University of Miami School of Medicine, Miami, Florida 33152

Nathan W. Shock, Gerontology Research Center, Baltimore City Hospitals, Baltimore, Maryland 21224

F. Marott Sinex, Department of Biochemistry, Boston University School of Medicine, Boston, Massachusetts 02118

Ruth B. Weg, University of Southern California, Ethel Percy Andrus Gerontology Center, Los Angeles, California 90007

David L. Wilson, Department of Physiology and Biophysics, University of Miami School of Medicine, Miami, Florida 33152

Tom M. Yau, Ohio Mental Health and Mental Retardation Center, Cleveland, Ohio 44107

Bert M. Zuckerman, Laboratory of Experimental Biology, University of Massachusetts, East Wareham, Massachusetts 02538

PREFACE

For a considerable number of years, scientists "discovering" aging as an area of research interest for the first time, have proposed theories based on extremely limited evidence, at best, or on inference, hypothesis, and even pure speculation. On the other hand, over the past two decades, a considerable number of capable experimental scientists studying aging in various areas of biology and medicine, have proposed, each in his own right, a variety of different theories of aging. These have ranged from the concept of purely genetic control of the aging process to more narrow viewpoints like the primary role of autoimmunity in aging, to that of the primary importance of cumulative, adverse environmental assaults and insults, resulting ultimately in the death of the organism.

This, the fourth publication of the proceedings of a series of annual symposia, held under the aegis of the Training Program in Cellular Aging of the Departments of Physiology/Biophysics and Microbiology of the University of Miami, includes the presentations of a group of scientists, all of whom have made major contributions to the field of biological gerontology. In actual fact, each of these individuals has come to an arena of interchange rather than one of controversy in presenting highly competent experimental data. As the reader will see, therefore, each case suggests an aspect of the aging process. As such, the presentations, as well as the overview by Dr. Ruth B. Weg in reflecting upon the tone as well as the major thrusts of the various presentations, should lead the reader, as it must have the audience attending the symposium, to the logical conclusion that the process of aging, like many other life processes of the total organism, is a highly complex and multifaceted phenomenon. At the same time, it is well worth emphasizing the recommendation by Dr. Andres, in his presentation, of the continuing need for a highly critical approach in studying aging in *all* organisms, as he has shown to be particularly true for the study of aging in man. It is hoped, therefore, that the various chapters of this volume will serve to motivate the entry into this ever growing, fascinating field of biological research, of additional, competent scientists from all areas of biology, medicine, and the physical sciences, as well.

ACKNOWLEDGMENTS

I must express special thanks to Mrs. Estella Cooney for her dedication and attention in producing a virtually unblemished camera copy for this publication. To Marvin L. Sussman, Associate Editor, and Dr. Jeffrey A. Chesky, Assistant Editor. I am also grateful for their efforts in the joint editing of not only the manuscripts but also the final camera copy of this publication.

The Training Program expresses its gratitude and appreciation to Dr. Alfred T. Sapse, President of Rom-Amer Pharmaceuticals, Ltd. of Beverly Hills, California, and to the Mead Johnson & Company Research Center, whose contributions helped make this conference successful and the publication of its proceedings possible.

The Symposium from which this publication resulted was supported for the most part by funds from the National Institute of Child Health and Human Development Training Program in Cellular Aging, Grant No. HD 00142, and, in part, by the University of Miami Department of Physiology and Biophysics, Professor Werner R. Loewenstein, Chairman.

Morris Rockstein, Ph.D.

THE GENETIC BASIS FOR LONGEVITY

Morris Rockstein

Department of Physiology and Biophysics
University of Miami School of Medicine
Miami, Florida

Although my primary interest in the field of aging
has been to establish first the facts of the aging process,
as it were, and then the mechanisms underlying a particular
aspect of aging. My interest in the basis for longevity
was heightened by the observation of the sex differential
in longevity favoring the female in the common house fly
as well as in two strains of white rats, during well over
a decade of the study of the biochemical bases for aging
of striated muscle.

THE STATISTICAL FACTS OF LONGEVITY

Life insurance statistics, shown in Table I, clearly
indicate that the percentage of actual to expected deaths
is always greater where both parents have died at a young
age. For example, where both parents have died for offspring still living, in the age group of 20-29, this expectancy is 121.2% versus 94% where both parents are still
living, for this same age group. On the other hand, where
both parents have died, for the offspring of age group
50-64, this percentage is 104% versus 73% for the same age
groups where both parents are still living. In figures 1a
and 1b, similarly, it is evident that for subjects under
60 years of age, where both parents have died, the curve
has shifted considerably to the left (curve B), indicating
a higher death rate than for such age groups where both
parents are still living; this is true for life insurance
statistics from two entirely different life insurance
companies.

1

TABLE I

MORTALITY AMONG INSURED MEN CLASSIFIED ACCORDING TO SURVIVORSHIP OF PARENTS WHEN INSURANCE WAS ISSUED; RATIOS OF ACTUAL TO EXPECTED DEATHS BASED ON CONTEMPORANEOUS MORTALITY EXPERIENCE OF ALL MALE LIVES

Issues 1899 to 1905 Traced to Policy Anniversary in 1939, Metropolitan Life Insurance Company, Ordinary Department

Age Group at Issue of Insurance	Percent of Actual to Expected Deaths		
	Both Parents Living	One Parent Living	Both Parents Dead
20–64	88.4	97.7	110.8
20–29	94.0	106.9	121.2
30–39	88.8	101.9	115.6
40–49	78.5	91.9	111.8
50–64	73.3	84.6	104.1

From: Dublin, L. I., Lotka, A. J. and Spiegelman, M.(1949). "Length of Life, A Study of the Life Table." Chapter 6, The Ronald Press, New York.

In a very interesting study, Alexander Graham Bell (1918), a genealogist by avocation, determined the relationship of offspring longevity to that of the parents for over 2200 male and 1800 female descendants of William Hyde. Thus, as shown in Table II, where both parents died at an age greater than 80, the average life span of 184 descendants was 52.7 years, or 20 years greater than that for 128 descendants from parents both of whom died at an age less than 60.

EVIDENCE FROM SEX DIFFERENCES IN LONGEVITY

In an early study, made well over 20 years ago, while involved in exploring the possible biochemical basis for insect resistance to insecticides, I was impressed with the fact that male house flies of the NAIDM strain showed a consistently shorter life span than the female as well as an accelerated rate of aging of the motor function of flight. As shown in figure 2, one can see that, for a

2

male house fly, the L50 is approximately 16 days of age
which, incidently, is very close to the mean value as well,
whereas the L50 for the female is well over 30 days of
age. In each case, both groups were allowed to feed <u>ad</u>
<u>libitim</u> on a full diet of sugar, powdered whole milk and
water, as adults (Rockstein and Lieberman, 1959).

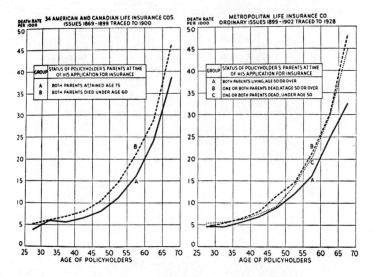

Fig. 1a and 1b Inheritance of Longevity. Death
rates at successive ages among white male policyholders
classified according to longevity of parents. (From:
Dublin, L. I., Lotka, A. J. and Spiegelman, M. (1949).
"Length of Life, A Study of the Life Table." Chapter 6,
The Ronald Press, New York.)

Even more interesting was the fact that, in a study
on the possible role of diet in determining longevity, it
was found that, for a limited diet of sugar and water only
(versus the complete powdered whole milk, sugar and water
diet) there was little if any effect upon the L50 in the
case of the male house flies (see figure 3a) whereas in
the case of the female (see figure 3b) there was a definite
diminution in life span (approaching that of the male) for
female adults reared on sugar and water alone (Rockstein
and Lieberman, 1959).

3

TABLE II

Showing the influence of a considerable degree of longevity in both father and mother upon the expectation of life of the offspring. (After Bell). (In each cell of the table the open figure is the average duration of life of the offspring and the bracketed figure is the number of cases upon which the average is based).

Father's age at death	Mother's age at death		
	Under 60	60–80	Over 80
Under 60	32.8 years (128)	33.4 years (120)	36.3 years (74)
60–80	35.8 (251)	38.0 (328)	45.0 (172)
Over 80	42.3 (131)	45.5 (206)	52.7 (184)

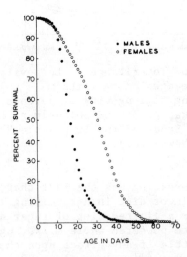

Fig. 2   Survival curves for male and female house flies.

4

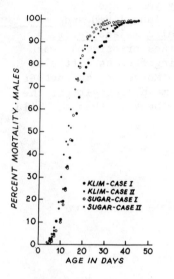

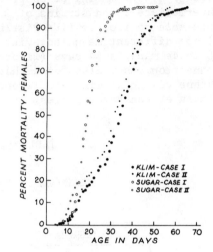

Fig. 3a The effect
of diet on male house
fly longevity.

Fig. 3b The effect
of diet on female house
fly longevity.

In the case of numerous other strains and species of
multicellular animals, sex differences in longevity favoring the female is almost a universally observed phenomenon
(Rockstein, 1958). This is not only true in humans (as
shown in Table III and Table IV) but also for such species
of animals as the white rat; the water flea, Daphnia; the
black widow spider; and a number of insect species including the house fly.

EVIDENCE FROM SPECIES-SPECIFIC LIFE SPANS

It is a well known fact, as shown in Tables III and
IV, that the mean and maximum life spans for a number of
species of animals either by sex or not, is fairly consistent for various species or strains of animals established
for numerous purposes of biomedical research, regardless
of the location of the laboratory, provided that conditions
of rearing and maintaining are fairly uniform. A very
interesting aspect of this line of evidence is the fact

that Pearl and Parker (1922a, b) many years ago, by brother-sister mating of short-lived, long-lived and intermediate-lived strains of <u>Drosophila</u> <u>melanogaster</u>, were able to isolate five distinct lines or strains, each with a different mean longevity ranging from as little as 14 to as many as 44 days (figure 4). Moreover, in another connection, they also found that the mean longevity of the mutant vestigial wing was lower, sex for sex, than the wild strain of the same species.

TABLE III

LIFE EXPECTANCY (IN YEARS) IN HUMANS

COUNTRIES	MALE	FEMALE
CANADA (1955-'57)	67.61	72.92
UNITED STATES (1959)	66.5	73.0
ISRAEL (1959)	70.23	72.26
CZECOSLOVAKIA (1958)	67.23	72.30
DENMARK (1951-'55)	69.79	72.60
FRANCE (1959)	67.0	73.6
WEST GERMANY (1959-'60)	66.69	71.94
EAST GERMANY (1955-'58)	66.13	70.68
UNITED KINGDOM (1959)	68.1	73.8
NORTHERN IRELAND (1958-'60)	67.51	71.94
NEW ZEALAND (1955-'57)	68.20	73.00
AUSTRALIA (1953-'55)	67.14	72.75
USSR (1958-'59)	64.0	72.0
JAPAN (1959)	65.21	69.88

TABLE IV

SEX DIFFERENCES IN LIFE SPAN

Animals	Male	Female	Reference
Man U.S.A. (1901)	48.2 yrs.	51.1 yrs.	U.S.P.H.S.
(1951)	66.6	72.6	
Australia (1948)	66.1	70.6	
England and Wales (1951)	65.8	70.9	
Sweden (1945)	67.1	69.7	
India (1921-31)	26.9	26.6	
White rat Average	483 days	801 days	McCay, et al.,
Maximum	927	1189	
Average	712	773	Robertson, et al.,
Daphnia magna 18 °C.	38.6 days	44.7 days	MacArthur and
28 °C.	21.9	29.2	Baillie
Black Widow Spider	100 days	271 days	Deevey and Deevey
Mealworm	60 days	111 days	
Tribolium confusum	178 days	199 days	Pearl, et al.,
Drosophila melanogaster			
Normal	31 days	33 days	Pearl, Gowen
Vestigial	14	20	Pearl and Parker
House Fly	18 days	30 days	Rockstein
	42	60	

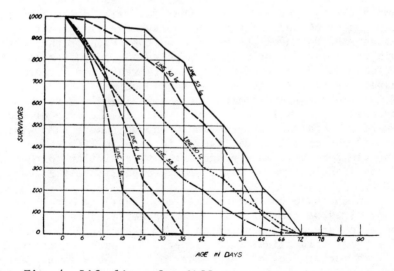

Fig. 4   Life lines for different inbred lines of descent in Drosophila. (From: Pearl, R. and Parker, S. L. (1922a). Am. Naturalist, Vol. 56, p. 174, The University of Chicago Press, Chicago, Illinois.)

Indeed, is it not amazing that the life expectancy of humans is virtually the same all over the world, namely somewhere around 66-68 years of age on the average for males, and 71-73 years of age for females (as shown in Table III)? Moreover, despite the fact that the life expectancy of males and females grouped together has actually increased due to many factors, especially the elimination of early postnatal and juvenile mortality, the maximum longevity of man has literally remained unchanged, since early times of recorded, authenticatable records which have been available to us, particularly in the last three centuries. Indeed, the only record of considerably over 110 to 112 years of age was that of a male Negro civil servant (purported to be more than 114 years of age, several years ago) who had been born a slave and whose birth records, at best, are subject to considerable question.

EVIDENCE FROM TWIN LONGEVITY DATA

Based on a study involving a population of 687 males and 907 females for adult twins over 60 years of age in the State of New York and surrounding areas, Kallman and Sander (1948) (Table V) found that for twins dying between the ages of 60 and 75 there was an average difference between the death of the second and the death of the first twin of 48 months for male twin pairs and only 24 months in the case of identical female twins (4 years and 2 years, respectively). In the case of non-identical (heterozygous) twins, there was a difference of approximately 9 years in the case of the males and over 7 years in the case of such female twin pairs. Interestingly enough, where the twins were of the opposite sex, the difference in life span for any twin pair gave an average value very similar to that of non-identical male twins, namely approximately 9 years apart.

In the same connection, Kallman (1957) in his later study cited several very interesting detailed case histories which are worth mentioning. For example, in the case of a pair of identical twin sisters, one pursuing a career as a farmer's wife and the mother of a sizable family and the other remaining single and earning a living in the city as a dressmaker, both of these ladies suffered massive cerebral hemorrhages on the very same day, although living apart, and died within 26 days of one another. He also

8

cited one particular case of identical male twins who died
on the same day at 86 years of age, this despite the fact
that no single case of fraternal or non-identical twin
pairs were found where the members of the twin pair died
closer than 90 days apart. In my own experience, the
husband of one of our secretaries died on a Saturday as a
result of a heart failure, the result of a chronic heart
condition. On the following Monday morning, a letter from
the wife of his identical twin brother in Jamaica arrived
in Miami announcing the death of his identical twin on the
very same, previous Saturday!

TABLE V

INTRA-PAIR DIFFERENCES IN LIFE SPAN
OF DECEASED TWIN PAIRS *

Age Group of First-Deceased Twin Partner	Average Intra-Pair Differences in Longevity in Months				
	Monozygotic Pairs		Same-Sexed Dizygotic Pairs		Opposite Sexed Pairs
	Male	Female	Male	Female	
60-75 yrs.	47.6	24.0	107.9	88.7	109.7
All pairs over 60 yrs.	47.6	29.4	89.1	61.3	126.6

* After Kallman and Sander, 1948.

In summary then, it is apparent, both from life
insurance statistics, intraspecies records, evidence from
sex differences favoring the female in most animal species,
as well as that from longevity data for identical versus
non-identical twins, that the primary basis for longevity
of an individual, strain, or a species is the genetic
material which is incorporated in the fertilized egg at the
climactic moment when the spermatozoon meets the unferti-
lized egg.

As such, as clearly shown in Table VI, life expectancy
of an individual, caucasian or otherwise, highly favors
the female up to the age 65 and that, furthermore, from
other evidence that the greatest insurance for long life is
to have had a long, continued line of ancestors of great,

average longevity and, furthermore, to have been born a female!

TABLE VI

	Expectation of Life* at Various Ages			
	White		Nonwhite	
Age	Male	Female	Male	Female
0	68.3	75.7	61.3	69.4
20	50.5	57.4	44.5	52.1
40	32.1	38.3	28.3	34.3
45	27.7	33.7	24.7	30.2
50	23.6	29.2	21.3	26.3
55	19.7	25.0	18.1	22.8
60	16.2	20.9	15.1	19.2
65	13.2	17.0	12.8	16.2
70	10.5	13.4	10.9	13.9

* Prepared from life expectancy data of the U. S. Department of Health, Education and Welfare, 1973 Life Insurance Fact Book.

REFERENCES

Bell, A. G. (1918). The Duration of Life and Conditions Associated with Longevity, A Study of the Hyde Genealogy. 57 pp. Washington, D. C. (privately printed).
Dublin, L. I., Lotka, A. J. and Spiegelman, M. (1949). "Length of Life, A Study of the Life Table". Revised edition, The Ronald Press, New York.
Kallman, F. J. (1957). Ciba Found. Colloq. on Ageing 3,131.
Kallman, F. J. and Sander, G. (1948). J. Heredity 39, 349.
Pearl, R. and Parker, S. L. (1922a). Am. Naturalist 56,174.
Pearl, R. and Parker, S. L. (1922b). Am. Naturalist 56,385.
Rockstein, M. (1958). J. Gerontol. 13, 7.
Rockstein, M. and Lieberman, H. M. (1959). Gerontologia 3, 23.

THE PROGRAMMED THEORY OF AGING

David L. Wilson

Department of Physiology and Biophysics
University of Miami
School of Medicine
Miami, Florida 33152

INTRODUCTION

"A theory is a species of thinking, and its right to exist is coextensive with its power of resisting extinction by its rivals." (T. H. Huxley, 1888, p. 312)

I will be dealing with the programmed theory of aging and its rivals. In a trivial sense, aging or senescence is obviously programmed since there is a predictable, species-specific pattern of changes which occurs as an organism grows older. However, the programmed theory of aging implies a good deal more than this. In the restricted sense of the theory, to speak of programming is to postulate a definite set or sequence of events which have been built into the organism through selective pressures. In other words, it is to postulate that there are direct or indirect selective advantages to limiting life span through senescence. In the absence of such programmed events, aging would not occur at all or it would occur later.

The programmed theory of aging does not specify a particular mechanism for aging. In this respect, it differs from a number of theories which will be discussed during this symposium. The theory is not a "how" theory so much as a "why" theory. Instead of concentrating on a particular mechanism or process for senescence, it tries to give, in evolutionary terms, reasons for the existence of aging.

The rival theories view senescence as occurring either because programming has reached an end or because, during the course of evolution, no way has been found to correct

certain kinds of wear-and-tear or certain kinds of errors
and waste build-up.

PROGRAMMED AGING: THE ARGUMENTS

It is accepted by many today that senescence is programmed in some species. Examples include annual plants,
salmon, lampreys, and many insect species. Therefore, in
a sense, we must determine whether these are special cases
or whether they are just the obvious examples of a more
general rule.

Alfred Russell Wallace was the first to propose that
selective pressures could favor senescence and death of
the individual because of overriding benefit for the
species:

> "...and thus we have the origin of old age,
> decay, and death; for it is evident that when
> one or more individuals have provided a
> sufficient number of successors they them-
> selves, as consumers of nourishment in a
> constantly increasing degree, are an injury to
> those successors. Natural selection therefore
> weeds them out, and in many cases favours such
> races as die almost immediately after they
> have left successors." (Weismann, 1889, p. 23)

August Weismann (1889) was the first to present a
detailed argument attempting to support the hypothesis of
programmed aging. Although his argument was not a valid
one, there are present-day arguments which stem from his
thoughts and which do appear to have some validity
(Medawar, 1957; Williams, 1957; Emerson, 1960; Smith, 1962;
Wynne-Edwards, 1962; and Guthrie, 1969). While Wallace
and Weismann both claimed a direct selective advantage for
senescence, most of these present-day theorists are only
willing to argue for indirect selective advantages, which
are derived from the hypothesis that the strength of
natural selection decreases with increasing age. This is
plausible, since the fewer the members of a population to
reach a given age, the less the impact of continued
reproduction will have on survival of the population. So
long as organisms are subject to accidental, random
causes of death, there will be fewer individuals surviving

12

to older and older ages. The fewer the number of
individuals surviving to a given age, the more reduced is
the strength of natural selection to counteract unfavorable
genes, whose negative effects become apparent only at later
ages.

Just to argue that the strength of natural selection
is reduced as the limit of normal life span in a population
is approached, would be to argue for a running-out-of-
programming. Thus, Medawar (1957) has proposed that one
solution which a species has to counteract the effects of
a deleterious gene, if it is not possible to eliminate it
through natural selection, is to postpone its time of
action. To the extent that natural selection leads to a
postponement of the effects of deleterious genes, there
will tend to be a piling-up of such harmful, programmed
effects toward the end of, or after, a normal life span for
the species.

In addition, Williams (1957) has argued that genes
exist with both favorable and unfavorable effects for the
individual. These would be pleiotrophic genes having more
than one effect. To the extent that the favorable effects
are able to increase reproductive capacity during youth,
the genes may still be selected for, so long as the deleterious effects are late enough in the life span of the
individual. To take a hypothetical example, suppose that
there is a hormone which reduces the chances of developing
arteriosclerosis, but which also is involved in the
production of the menstrual cycle. Now, if the selective
advantage of terminating reproductive capability at a
given time offset the disadvantage of increased risk of
arteriosclerosis later in life, there will then be a
selection for shutting-off the hormone's production. Of
course, the detrimental effect of enhanced likelihood of
arteriosclerosis may be overcome too, through further
mutation or variation, but there will be reduced selective
pressures leading to this, especially if the arteriosclerosis occurs late enough in normal life span. Williams'
argument is that the selective value of a gene depends
upon how it affects the total probability of reproduction
for an individual. Since there is an unavoidable decrease
in probability of survival to older ages due to random
accidental events, even without senescence, genes which
have delayed negative effects may still be advantageous.
Once one such gene is present in a population, other

13

pleiotrophic genes having deleterious effects at about the
same time or later in an individual's life span can be
selected-for more readily. Thus it would not be surprising if a number of effects in various organ systems were
to contribute to senescence, as a consequence of this kind
of accumulation of late-acting, deleterious genes.

The preceding arguments all point to the role of
indirect selective pressures in bringing about programmed
senescence in living organisms. As with the running-out-
of-program theory, these arguments involve multiple causes,
acting at about the same time to bring about senescence.

There are also arguments which defend the proposition
that direct selective pressures have brought about senescence. That is, in a given environment, every species is
postulated to have its own "best" average number of total
offspring which each pair should produce. In this way,
the chance for selection of each pair's genotypes can be
optimally balanced against the need to test other
variations. One reason for the existence of a limit on
the reproductive capacity of a given individual is that
any niche has a limit on the total number of individuals
which it can support at any one time without widespread
starvation or other similar catastrophe arising from
over-population. If individuals have longer life spans,
there must be fewer of them over any given period of time,
and thus fewer possible gene combinations. In contrast,
with a more limited life span, a species will be able to
support a larger variety of gene types during any period
of time and during population growth. This should lead to
an enhanced rate of evolution and an increased likelihood
of developing advantageous variants which can respond to
environmental change. At the other extreme, of course, if
the life span should become too short, then the chance of
a particular individual's offspring surviving to their
reproductive maturity becomes too small, and the more
classical considerations of selection for greater numbers
of offspring prevails. In short, the argument is that
there is an optimum average reproductive life span for
individual members of a species. This will depend upon a
number of factors, such as the time to reproductive
maturity, the number of offspring produced per mating,
the likelihood of an offspring surviving to reproductive
maturity, and the length of time between matings, etc.

One way in which reproductive life span may be

limited is through senescence; the other would be to
terminate reproduction without terminating life altogether.
In those individuals which do terminate reproduction at a
certain age, it is still advantageous to have senescence
occur, because post-reproductive individuals are a burden
for the species insofar as rate of evolution is concerned.
Post-reproductive individuals compete for the same niche
and could be replaced more profitably (in relation to the
rate of evolution) with younger, reproducing individuals.
Thus we would expect short post-reproductive life spans
to be the norm, unless there are overriding advantages,
such as (with humans) the need for extended care for offspring coupled with dangers to life caused by child-bear-
ing.
    Arguments similar to this have been presented by
Wynne-Edwards (1962):

> "It has long been widely assumed that natural
> selection will normally promote longevity of
> adult organisms since those that survive long-
> est are likely to make the largest total con-
> tribution to posterity, and their genes must
> consequently increase in frequency with succeed-
> ing generations.... It seems very much more
> probable that, in so far as the average potential
> life span in any species is physiologically
> fixed, its duration has been arrived at by
> selection, in the process of permitting the
> stock as a whole to survive; and that it is more
> or less completely integrated with other basic
> parameters of population balance, like fecundity."

The general criticism against such arguments for a direct
role for selective pressures in bringing about a programmed aging arise from those evolutionists who do not
believe that intergroup selection mechanisms operate, that
is, they limit themselves to selective pressures operating
at the individual level (Lack, 1965; Williams, 1966).
    Unfortunately, even with direct selective pressure
favoring senescence, there may still not be simple
(genetic) causes for aging. One would expect life span
determination to be multi-genic, the way that intelligence
or body size is, rather than controlled by a single gene.
This is especially likely since there would be a difference

in the rate at which the selective pressures at individual
and group levels can operate; in the short term, non-
senescing individuals will multiply disproportionately
within a population and be selected-for. In contrast,
over a longer span of time, and in competition with other
populations, the species with longer-lived individuals may
be at a disadvantage, and may be selected against. Of
course, a species could evolve a safeguard against this
possibility if aging were multi-genic and thus protected
from radical changes through mutations. Even if a single
gene evolved to control senescence in some species, it is
likely that the other, indirect selective pressures will
have led to other, deleterious gene effects being present
at the time of programmed senescence. The exception to
this rule might come in simpler systems, that is, organ
systems and cell lines which show early senescence relative
to the rest of an organism. Examples include mouse
placental giant cells and some cultured cell lines.

Again, even assuming the direct selective advantage
argument to be true, one way to bring about the senescence,
and thereby earlier death of an organism, is simply to
terminate the program. Rather than any specific, positive
event, running-out-of-program would serve the purpose of
limiting life span, and might have other selective
advantages (Guthrie, 1969). For example, in those
organisms which experience a single breeding season, in
the case of both plant and animal annuals, the selective
advantages, which such organisms possess because of
directing their "energies" at a given time towards reproduction, may more than offset the disadvantage of not
surviving (i.e., not being programmed to survive) the
following winter. This could easily be seen to be advantageous if the probability of an adult surviving the
winter were small even if some of its "energies" were
redirected for this purpose.

Nevertheless, the programmed theory does deal with
certain issues in aging which other theories, and especially those "how" theories (which depend upon "running-out-of-
program" or upon unrepairable "wear-and-tear" as a basis
for aging) have not adequately confronted. One such issue
consists of range of life spans. Even if one were to
eliminate insects (and others) as being special cases and
just examine the species-average life spans found among
mammals, one would find a hundred-fold range. Theories

such as the mutation theory, the autoimmune theory, the crosslinkage theory, the error-catastrophe theory, etc., must present reasons for the existence of such a wide range, if all of the species age by the same mechanism. What damaging processes are genetically uncorrectable in some rodents at one year of age but have been postponed in man for seventy times as long? If one includes other, non-mammalian species, the problem becomes compounded at least another hundred-fold.

In addition, if one rejects the premise of programmed aging, one may be forced to argue for ever-increasing reproductive life spans for all species; natural selection should forever be taking advantage of the natural varia- tions which exist in life span among the members of a species to select for those mutants with longer lives. If trapped into such a position, one might begin to wonder why most insects live only to a few weeks of age, why rodents haven't surpassed primates in longevity, and why tortoise and man have done so exceptionally well (especial- ly with man so dependent upon his non-renewable nerve cells).

If one attempts to argue for a running-out-of-program as being the cause of aging, and if one argues that this has happened because of the reduced selective pressures existing on reduced numbers of individuals living to older ages, then senescence in the wild should be a rare event; one would not expect to detect significant numbers of individuals showing any signs of senescence in a natural population. To the extent that senescence plays a significant role in death rates for a population, so should there also be significant selective pressure to lead to elimination or postponement of such senescence under this theory. However, it is now widely accepted that senescence does occur among some populations and that survival curves frequently show a shape intermediate between the exponential decline expected in a population not showing aging and the rectangular shape associated with demise from aging alone (Bourlière, 1959; Comfort, 1964). Indeed, one must be careful in arguing against senescence being manifest even in populations which show an exponential decline in numbers (indicating equal probability of dying per unit time) since even in this case senescence could be occurring but be offset by enhanced survival due to both learning and the development

17

of immunity to common diseases.

Of course, it is possible that, if senescence has no
significant effect on the life spans of members of a
species, programmed aging is not present. For these
species, the "ideal" life span might be longer than allowed
for by environmental conditions. When these species are
maintained in captivity, the observed senescence could
indeed be due to a running-out-of-program. In contract,
many of the larger, longer-lived mammals and birds have
survival curves which do indicate senescence, even among
wild populations. For these, the running-out-of-program
theory would require longer-lived variations to be
continually selected-for, and there should be an ever-
increasing duration of life for the succeeding generations
of such species. This does not appear to be the case, and
the programmed theory is more likely to hold for these
species.

AGING MECHANISMS

It is probably possible to subsume almost any of the
"how" theories of senescence under the programmed theory,
as there are many mechanisms whereby senescence could be
built into an organism. Even the mutation theory, with
the stipulation that some DNA repair mechanism be shut-off
to trigger senescence, could be incorporated as the
senescence mechanism programmed into an organism. However,
most of the arguments supporting a programmed senescence
would require that aging be an active process and would
require some positive event, some programmed act leading
to senescence. With today's knowledge of molecular
genetics and mechanisms of protein synthesis, there are
some mechanisms which are more likely than others. Most
developmental control mechanisms are thought to involve
controls on the portion of a genome capable of being
transcribed into RNAs and translated into proteins. If
aging is viewed as a continuation of developmental program,
the most likely senescence mechanism would involve a
shutting-off of the synthesis of specific proteins or
their corresponding mRNAs or would involve turning-on the
synthesis of new proteins detrimental to the organism.
Such a mechanism for snescence could produce rapid or
gradual senescence. For example, blocking the synthesis
of a mRNA would cause a decrease in the synthesis of the

18

corresponding protein. The time-course of the decrease would depend upon the half-life of the remaining mRNA species. This could be hours or years. The actual time-course of the physiological manifestations of aging would depend on the roles of the proteins and their own half-lives. There is no end to the complexities or multiple manifestations which could be programmed. Nevertheless, it should be clear that the key to senescence would not lie in attempting to understand and correct the outward manifestations, one at a time, but in getting to the underlying control mechanism itself.

The kind of experiment most likely to be conclusive in this respect would be a genetic analysis of aging. One approach would be by the isolation and study of mutants which have either significantly shorter or significantly longer average life spans. By such a study, one can hope to obtain direct information concerning the kind of mechanisms actually operating in aging. Other kinds of experiments which focus on the physiological and biochemical manifestations of aging are likely to remain bogged-down in complexity, if aging is programmed for the species being studied. For such a genetic study, one would choose an organism having a short generation time and allowing large numbers to be maintained easily. The selection would entail continuing to choose those individuals with longer and longer reproductive life spans. Unfortunately, as I have previously indicated, these may not be common mutants. Once obtained, the mutants would have to be analyzed, and this would be the complex part of the research program; not all such mutants would involve the basic mechanism of aging itself. Nevertheless, I believe that this kind of approach to the problem is likely to be the most fruitful.

CONCLUSIONS

It has not been my intention to prove that the programmed theory of aging is universally true, but that it may be more widely applicable than many have thought it to be. It is probably most dangerous to assert any one of these "why" theories as being general, be it the pro-grammed theory, the running-out-of-program theory, a theory involving wear-and-tear, or one involving error and waste build-up. Undoubtedly, different theories are more likely to be valid for different species. To that extent, any attempt to assert a "how" or mechanism theory as general will be equally dangerous.

When it comes to aging in whole organisms, all of the arguments supporting a programmed theory of aging point toward senescence being a complex process involving the interplay of a number of genes. This is not a very hopeful situation for those who wish to extend human life span. A consideration of the alternative of a running-out-of-program as being the cause of aging, presents even less hope for overcoming senescence, because of the large number of modifications in all organ systems which would be required to prolong life significantly. Thus, predictions of a soon-to-be-realized, scientifically-generated fountain of youth (Rosenfeld, 1973) are embarrassingly optimistic.

We can hope that science and medicine will extend the period of useful, productive life, especially for those not now reaching 70 or 80 years of age. Beyond that, our hereditary predispositions are liable to continue to determine our life spans more than new scientific knowledge will. Insofar as useful life span is concerned, it is society, with its present attitudes and treatment of many individuals over 65 years of age, which exhibits as much that needs correcting as the elderly individuals themselves (De Beauvoir, 1972).

To be able to overcome human aging in this time of approaching overpopulation would entail an even further decrease in birth rate and a slowing of human evolution. We are a long way from extending human life span significantly, and perhaps this is for the best. With the population which we already have, one can imagine the crisis which would have arisen if Ponce De Leon actually had found his fountain of youth here in Florida. As it is, we can take some small comfort in the fact that by our personal deaths we also make room for a new individual. Each generation has its three-score-and-ten to make the world a better place in which to live and to make all of life more worth living

ACKNOWLEDGEMENT

I thank Margaret G. Wilson for helpful comments on the manuscript.

REFERENCES

Bourlière, F. (1959). In "The Lifespan of Animals" (G.E.W. Wolstenholme and M. O'Connor, eds.), CIBA Found. Colloq. on Aging, Vol. 5, p. 90.

Comfort, A. (1964). "Ageing: The Biology of Senescence." Routledge and Kegan Paul, London.

De Beauvoir, S. (1972). "The Coming of Age." Putnam, N.Y.

Emerson, A.E. (1960). In "Evolution After Darwin" (S. Tax, ed.), Vol. 1, pp. 307-348, University of Chicago Press, Chicago.

Guthrie, R.D. (1969). Perspect. Biol. Med. 12, 313.

Huxley, T.H. (1888). "Science and Culture." MacMillan, London.

Lack, D. (1965). J. Ecology 53, 237.

Medawar, P.B. (1957). "The Uniqueness of the Individual." Methuen and Co., London.

Rosenfeld, A. (1973). Sat. Review of the Sciences 1, No. 2, 46.

Smith, J.M. (1962). Proc. Roy. Soc. B 157, 115.

Weismann, A. (1889). "Essays Upon Heredity and Kindred Biological Problems." Oxford University Press, London.

Williams, G.C. (1957). Evolution 11, 398.

Williams, G.C. (1966). "Adaptation and Natural Selection." Princeton University Press, Princeton.

Wynne-Edwards, V.C. (1962). "Animal Dispersion in Relation to Social Behavior." Hafner, N. Y.

THE MUTATION THEORY OF AGING

F. Marott Sinex, Ph.D.

Department of Biochemistry
Boston University School of Medicine
Boston, Massachusetts 02118

In this presentation, I find myself in an unusual position of defending a single theory of aging, namely that aging is the result of somatic mutations. Let me say at the outset that I do not believe that human aging is the result of any single primary cause. There is no particular evolutionary incentive for this to be the case. Furthermore, it may be very difficult to distinguish clearly primary and secondary causes, since the deteriorative changes which occur in aging reinforce each other. As a chemist, I seek a mechanistic "how" and the approach which I find myself coming back to again and again is that of spontaneous mutation and its measurement.

What do we know about the rate of spontaneous mutation? In the germ line it is low. The human germ line probably accumulates 0.1 to 0.5 mutations per generation so that the mutation rate per gene is in the order of 1×10^{-5} per life time or something like 4×10^{-11} mutations per hour per gamete (Stern, 1973). There may be a good deal of selection in these haploid cells. Only a small fraction of the ova are released by the ovaries and only the fittest of the sperm may effectively carry out a fertilization.

In contrast to haploid gametes, somatic cells are diploid. It is probable that most aging "hits" are dominant, not recessive. The belief that aging hits are dominant is based primarily on the observations of Lamb and Maynard-Smith (1964) and Harris (1971) that the effect of ionizing radiation on cells is more consistent with the assumption that radiation injury is dominant or epigenetic and not recessive. This is an extremely important point. The alternative position of Szilard (1959), that aging hits

are recessive and are only important when a cell becomes
homozygous for a mutation as a consequence of an aging hit,
is not tenable. I believe that aging hits are relatively
common, modifying and unbalancing cellular control and
function, but not necessarily destroying enzymes. The
majority of these hits probably occur in control genes and
not the genes which code for actual enzyme structure per
se, because the former are more numerous than the latter.

Even though the effects of aging hits are random at a
molecular level, those genes which cause vulnerability to
these random molecular events in a particular species, may
be highly specific and limited, a point made by George
Sacher (1973).

Attempts have been made to measure the rate of spontaneous mutation in human fibroblasts in culture. Albertini
and DeMars (1973) used the appearance of clones insensitive
to 8-azaguanine, a compound which is converted enzymatical-
ly into a cytotoxic nucleotide. If the enzyme mutates,
the cells are no longer injured. Albertini and DeMars
reported a mutation rate of 4.5×10^{-6} per cell per tissue
culture generation. If the body contains something like
30 billion cells, then the average cell has gone fewer
than 34 generations of divisions. If one assumes that the
rate of mutation in the body is similar to that in tissue
culture, then the average number of mutations per cell in
the organism would be approximately three. Albertini and
DeMars do not indicate the time necessary in order to
culture a generation of cells; however, the mutation rate
per hour must be of the order of 1×10^{-7} per hour. This
would generate a mutation rate per cell on a time basis
over a lifetime of more than a thousand. Such high rates
of mutation might indeed impair function. If the activity
of an average enzyme was depressed 10 per cent because of
a mutation, the total number of mutations per cell would
again be quite high, something less than 20,000.

Until now, we have been discussing irreparable mutations. The fact that an aging hit is not repaired is what
makes it significant. Reparable injury may be of little
ultimate significance, but is important to discuss because
we believe that this is the type of injury which rates of
repair measure. The hydrolysis of the phosphate diester
bonds of DNA is the most likely event to occur at 37° C
with the passage of time. DNA would be highly susceptible
to hydrolysis if it were single-stranded. The fact that it

is double-stranded confers upon it considerable chemical
stability. Nevertheless, small fractions of DNA are open
at any instance and this breathing may be sufficient to
lead to spontaneous hydrolysis which must be repaired if
the genetic information is to be retained. Admirably suit-
ed to make such repairs is the system of repair enzymes in
the body, consisting of endonucleases, repair polymerase
and ligase (which rebuilds a single strand gap using the
information in the complimentary strand). There may also
be a small amount of depurination and oxidation of deoxy-
ribofuranose rings in the regions which are repaired.

Exposure to chronic, low level irradiation may mimic
some aspects of aging in animals. Such animals have altered life tables and have tissues which appear older in many
ways. However, radiation injury is not identical with
aging. For example, it is relatively easy to tell a
radiation-induced cataract from an age-related cataract.
Aging does not wipe out platelets. However, there are even
theoretical reasons for considering the action of ionizing
radiation and aging to be similar. In water, ionizing
radiation forms hydrogen radical ($\cdot$H), hydroxyl radical
($\cdot$OH) and hydrated electrons (e$^-$aq). These hydrated
electrons can react with molecular oxygen, O_2, to form
superoxide radical ($\cdot O_2^-$). Superoxide radical reacts with
a proton to become perhydroxyl radical ($\cdot HO_2$).

e.g., ionizing radiation

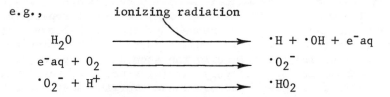

$$H_2O \longrightarrow \cdot H + \cdot OH + e^-aq$$
$$e^-aq + O_2 \longrightarrow \cdot O_2^-$$
$$\cdot O_2^- + H^+ \longrightarrow \cdot HO_2$$

During normal metabolism the reduction of oxygen
through single electron transfer by certain oxidases
(xanthine oxidase being the classical example) produces
superoxide, the same superoxide produced by ionizing radiation (Misra and Fridovich, 1972). Superoxide and an ex-
cited form of oxygen known as singlet oxygen are probably
the active forms of oxygen to be considered when speaking
of any "free radical" theory of aging. Superoxide is de-
composed into oxygen and peroxide by the enzyme superoxide
dismutase and the peroxide is then destroyed by catalase.
The enzyme superoxide dismutase, may play an important role

in controlling the rate of aging in the body. We believe
that superoxide and superoxide dismutase are potentially
more important in aging than the peroxides and peroxidase
built into older forms of the free radical approach.
Assigning a more primary role to superoxide and superoxide
dismutase does not negate subsequent events visualized in
the free radical theory as to the importance of auto-
oxidation and the accumulation of autoxidized-lipid.

Not all genes code enzymes. It is quite possible that
more genes are involved in control of other genes and differentiation than in the direct coding of enzymes. In many
instances an enzyme may control its own expression, directly through its regulatory gene (known as autogenous re-
pression) or indirectly through metabolic products which
serve as repressors or inducers. A somatic mutation may,
therefore, either decrease the functional effectiveness of
an enzyme directly or switch it from a regulated enzyme to
constituitive enzyme. If the mutation occurs in a regulatory site as opposed to a site coding for a structural
enzyme, the concentration of the enzyme may increase or
decrease depending on whether (in its regulatory role) the
enzyme acts as an inducer or repressor. This switching of
regulated to constituitive status may at times express
itself as a dedifferentiation and a lack of or sluggishness
in response to hormonal and regulatory control. The variation among individual cells in a tissue would increase
with age and this is what is actually observed.

I now wish to discuss the significance of repair in
aging and I have already exposed my hand. I believe that
the majority of repair is used to correct rather simple
spontaneous injury, primarily the spontaneous hydrolysis of
DNA. There are several very careful studies of the levels
of repair in the literature. These, for the most part,
have served as controls in studies of the repair of injury
from ultraviolet or ionizing radiation.

While Caren Gundberg, in our laboratory, has attempted
to measure the amount of strand breakage in the DNA of
older animals, using a sucrose gradient in an ultracentri-
fuge, the anticipated number of broken strands associated
with aging injury probably cannot be detected by the use of
this method. However, repairable repair, if not aging
injury itself, can be measured in tissue culture using
thymidine incorporation into cells whose DNA synthesis for
replication purposes is inhibited. By incorporating

26

bromodeoxyuridine in the media, accumulated segments repaired over a period of time can be rebroken in longer ultraviolet radiation. These accumulated breaks can be measured on an alkaline sucrose gradient. Estimates of repair using such procedures give high values for the amounts of repair considerably exceeding reasonable estimates of the rates of spontaneous mutation. Indeed, it is quite possible that, in brain, the DNA of neurones which we usually think of as being stable for a lifetime is actually turned over several times in the human species by repair. Table I summarizes the details of this discussion to this point.

The last column, "Bases per base pair per hour" is an attempt to produce a number through which to compare repair and mutation. From this last column we infer that:

1. the rate of somatic mutation appreciably exceeds that of the germ line,

2. the rate of somatic mutation is sufficient to account for functional loss in individual cells of an aging organism,

3. loss in enzyme activity in an organism such as Dr. Gershon's nematodes could be due to somatic mutation (Gershon and Gershon, 1970). (Let me hasten to add that this is not my explanation for his observation, but this is another subject.),

4. the rate of repair greatly exceeds any reasonable value of the rate of mutation (and, in our opinion, primarily reflects the repair of easily repairable sites of little significance in aging).

As I have indicated earlier, chronic low lever radiation injury is a good model for aging. However, what compounds the problem is the fact that ionizing radiation is more effective than aging "hits" in producing chromosomal breaks (Curtis, 1963; Curtis and Miller, 1971). Such major injury as broken chromosomes are often eliminated in subsequent cell divisions through cell death and thus may not contribute to long-term functional loss. If injury from ionizing radiation and aging were identical, then long-lived species should be resistant to radiation injury,

27

TABLE I

Estimates of Mutation by Different Methods*

METHOD	Mutations per cell per generation	Mutations per gene per generation	Mutations per gene per hour	Bases per base pair per hour
Gametes	$\boxed{1 \times 10^{-1}}$	1×10^5	4×10^{-11}	3×10^{-16}
Tissue Culture (3)	1.4×10^3	$\boxed{4 \times 10^{-6}(\text{cell})}$ 7×10^{-2}	1×10^{-7}	6×10^{-11}
Enzyme	2×10^3	$\boxed{1 \times 10^{-1}}$	2×10^{-7}	1×10^{-12}
Repair	1×10^{10}	5×10^5	8×10^{-1}	$\boxed{5 \times 10^{-6}}$

*In this table the more primary data are enclosed in boxes. Human cells and life spans are assumed. A gamete is assumed to have 10,000 genes with a reproductive life span of 30 years. Otherwise, the number or genes is taken as 20,000 and the life span as 75 years. Repair is based on the tissue culture data of Albertini and DeMars (1973). The enzyme figures assume 10 per cent mutation per life time.

whereas they are not. Man is more sensitive to ionizing radiation than the rodent. There is another paradox, however, and that is that the efficiency of the repair of radiation injury, while not well correlated with radiation sensitivity, is somewhat better correlated with longevity. As an exceptionally long-lived species, man is better at excising thymidine dimers than rodents. The human species must certainly be better at something concerned with aging, since we live 25-30 times as long as rodents.

Table II demonstrates this aging-ionizing radiation paradox, namely that many short-lived species have an extraordinary resistance to ionizing radiation.

TABLE II

Approximate LD_{50} for Ionizing Radiation

	r
Spermatogonia	50
Man	450
Mouse	550
Rat	750
Rat (chronic low level dose)	2,100
Goldfish	2,300
Drosophila (adult)	64,000
Paramecia	300,000

This table demonstrates the lack of correlation between radiation sensitivity and longevity. Drosophila and Paramecia are short-lived, but radiation resistant. Man is long-lived, but relatively sensitive to ionizing radiation.

Thus, we believe that there are three types of mutation; spontaneous hydrolysis, radiation-induced and aging.
These vary in their qualitative and quantitative properties; spontaneous hydrolysis being highly repairable, and
radiation injury being somewhat less so. Both these types
of mutation have some significance in aging. Aging hits,
on the other hand, have a low level of reparability and
are highly significant in aging.

I therefore believe that the repair of somatic mutations is of importance in the aging of a particular group
of species, to one of which we belong. Such species are
relatively long-lived, two years or more, and reasonably
radiation sensitive, showing a 50 per cent lethal with less
than 3,000 r.

Much of what we know about repair is in terms of the
repair of thymidine dimers induced by ultraviolet radiation. This is because the excision of thymidine dimers
can readily be measured. We know less about the ability
of repair systems to deal with limited miscoding, such as
point mutations, insertions, deletions and inversions.

The study of the repair of mutations induced by nitrous acid would seem important. Here there is a type of
point mutation that might easily be brought about by other
free radical mechanisms. For example:

Adenine, which bonds to thymine, loses an amino group
and becomes hypoxanthine, which codes for cytosine,

Guanine, which bonds to cytosine, loses an amino group
and changes to xanthine which codes for cytosine, consequently the error is not propagated,

Cytosine, which bonds to guanine, becomes thymine,
which codes for adenine, whereas

Thymine, is unaffected by nitrous acid.

It is my feeling that most species which age because
of somatic mutation also have cancer. I believe the reason
for this is that the activation of oncogenic virus is
associated with efforts to repair aging hits.

I do not believe that the somatic mutation theory is
incompatible with other approaches to aging. The molecular
injury itself is not what kills us. It is the vulnerabil-

ity of the species to such fairly random molecular events.
The rate of mutation may, in turn, be influenced by other
factors affecting cell activity. Functional loss and cell
death impair homeostasis and slow us down and make us less
capable. And, as I stated at the beginning of my presentation, it is sometimes difficult to distinguish between
that which is primary and that which is secondary in relation to processes in something as complex as a living
organism.

REFERENCES

Albertini, R. J. and DeMars, R. (1973). Mutation Res. 18,
    197.
Curtis, H. J. (1963). Science 141, 686.
Curtis, H. J. and Miller, K. (1971). J. Gerontol. 26, 292.
Gershon, H. and Gershon, D. (1970). Nature 227, 1241.
Harris, M. (1971). J. Cell Physiol. 78, 177.
Lamb, M. J. and Maynard-Smith, J. (1964). Exp. Gerontol.
    1, 11.
Misra, H. P. and Fridovich, L. (1972). J. Biol. Chem. 247,
    188.
Sacher, G. (1973). Personal communication.
Stern, C. (1973). "Principles of Human Genetics." Freeman,
    San Francisco.
Szilard, L. (1959). Proc. Nat. Acad. Sci. U.S. 45, 30.

AN "AUTOIMMUNE" THEORY OF AGING

William H. Adler

Laboratory of Cellular and Comparative Physiology
Gerontology Research Center
National Institute of Child Health & Human Development
PHS, U.S. Department of Health, Education and Welfare
Bethesda, Maryland
and the Baltimore City Hospitals
Baltimore, Maryland 21224

This discussion will deal with an autoimmune theory of aging. It will neither be a review of evidence to support this theory, nor an all encompassing view of immune function in aging. What I shall attempt to do is to deal with the evidence on autoimmune phenomena, immune-function, and the pathology of aging; and will propose a unifying hypothesis to link this evidence both as phenomena and as a cause of aging and age-associated disease.

The autoimmune theory of aging outlined by Walford (1969) simply states that autoimmunity with associated auto-antibody are crucial in determining cell death or cell changes which lead to the aging process. There is certainly an association of auto-antibody and age, but is there a direct causal relationship and is there good evidence that the disease process in aging is causally related to the auto-antibody? There are many problems in linking these phenomena. Perhaps the first problem to be considered is the actual event which could initiate auto-antibody appearance. If it is simply the escape of a clone of cells from control, then one must consider the possible control mechanism and the escape itself. A control mechanism is obscure and to hypothesize a system of individual control mechanisms for each specific antibody produced in which only the one that prevents auto-immunity is the one which is turned off, is difficult to defend (Makinodan et al., 1973). Accordingly, one is faced with the "escape", that is, the appearance of cells synthesizing and releasing

antibody with specificity to "self" tissue or serum components. The explanation of this event must, of necessity,
take into account the real possibility that the causative
event which leads to auto-antibody appearance has additional effects on other organs and tissues other than just a
small number of immunocompetent cells in the lymphoreticu-
lar system. This event, which turns on the appearance of
auto-antibody, could also conceivably be the cause of the
tissue damage which has been thought to be caused by the
auto-antibody.

Could the escape event be a mutation in an isolated
lymphoid cell? The answer must be evaluated in terms of
the frequency of this mutation. The appearance of auto-
antibody in older individuals is a very common event
(Hallgren et al., 1973); therefore the mutation would be
very common, and this frequency, which is difficult to
explain, has no precedent. Furthermore, it would be
equally possible that cellular mutation in other organs or
tissues would be occurring and could itself be a cause of
aging. However, one is still faced with explaining or
assigning cause to the high incidence of auto-antibody in
advanced age. Before going into a possible mechanism of
the cause for this antibody, let me first briefly outline
the changes in the immune system that can be seen in the
aging process.

In the measurement of immune function one can look at
the synthesis of antibody as a function of the humoral
immune system. When one does this, one finds a decline of
antibody synthesis in aged humans and mice. In general,
however, the humoral immune system remains at a functionally normal level for a large part of the lifetime in
animals and humans (Heidrick and Makinodan, 1972), especially if one examines the response to antigens which do
not require thymic function. The time of the decline of
antibody production capacity usually occurs after the
onset of the aging process (figure 1).

To measure the function of the cellular immune system
is more difficult because other factors figure into the
possible errors or artifacts that could occur and obscure
a measure of lymphocyte function. For instance, delayed
skin test reactivity depends on the ability of the animal
species to manifest a measurable skin reaction. Not all
animal species manifest good skin test delayed hypersensitivity and so animal models evaluated on this basis are

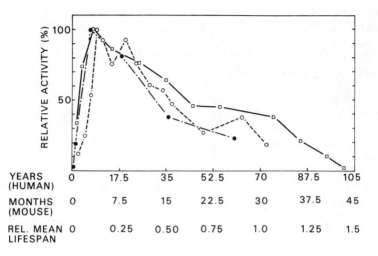

Fig. 1 Decrease in antibody formation in aging humans and mice. □———□ Human anti-A isohemagglutinin titers (Thomsen and Kettel, 1929). ●——● Mouse (C3H/ANf Cum X 101/Cum F_1 mice) peak serum agglutinin response to skeep red blood cell antigen stimulation (Makinodan and Peterson, 1964). o----o Mouse peak serum agglutinin response to rat RBC antigen stimulation by adoptively transferred mouse spleen cells (Makinodan and Peterson, 1964).

difficult. A second consideration is the antigen needed to induce delayed hypersensitivity, in that an antigen which induces good antibody production usually induces a poor, delayed hypersensitivity reaction (Parish and Liew, 1972). In the evaluation of humans the choice of antigen is limited and, as a consequence, the experimental results are scant. However, it can be shown that skin test delayed reactivity does decrease with age (Giannini and Sloan, 1957; Waldorf et al., 1968). Another way to approach the measure of lymphocyte function or the cellular immune system, which avoids the necessity to allergize with an antigen or deal with the problem of species variation in skin test demonstrability, is to evaluate the lymphocyte function in an in vitro tissue culture situation. There are several possibilities for approaching this problem. One is to measure the mitogenic response of lymphocytes

35

from lymphoid tissues exposed to mitogens in vitro. The choice of mitogen allows a measure of proliferative ability of different classes of lymphoid cells, in that, thymic-derived lymphocytes can be shown to be responsive to the mitogenic effects of phytohemagglutinin (PHA) (Takiguchi et al., 1971).

By assessing the response to PHA one can make some assumptions concerning the number or mitotic potential of a class of lymphocytes that are functionally important in cell-mediated immune function. From figure 2, it can be seen that as early in life of an A/J mouse as one year of age, the T cell reactivity is virtually non-existent. This is true in the spleen cell population as well as the thymus cell population.

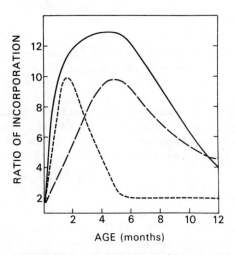

Fig. 2 In vitro responses of A/J spleen cells and thymus cells to various mitogenic stimuli. ——— PHA induced ^{3}H-thymidine incorporation in A/J spleen cell cultures (Peavy et al., 1974). ----- PHA induced ^{3}H-thymidine incorporation in A/J thymus cell cultures (Peavy et al., 1974). — — — Allogeneic cell (C57BL/6) induced ^{3}H-thymidine incorporation in A/J spleen mixed cell cultures (Adler et al., 1971). Ratio of incorporation is the figure obtained by dividing the counts per minute (cpm) in the stimulated cultures by the cpm in the non-stimulated control cultures.

However, if one studies a long-lived mouse strain, the T cell reactivity remains at a high level until later in life than in the A/J mouse (Hori et al., 1973) (figure 3). Another response that can be quantitated is the response to the stimulation of alloantigens in the so-called mixed lymphocyte reaction. In this reaction, the ability of a class of thymic-derived lymphoid cells to recognize and respond to a foreign set of histocompatability antigens, i.e., cell-associated antigens, can be assessed.

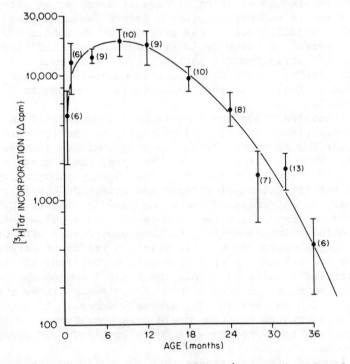

Fig. 3 PHA stimulation of (C57BL/6 X C3H) F-1 spleen cells from mice of different ages. The ^{3}H-thymidine incorporation is expressed as the cpm in the stimulated cultures minus the cpm in the control cultures (Hori et al., 1973).

When one makes these various measurements and looks at the effects of age on the reactivity of T (thymic-derived lymphocyte) or MLC (mixed lymphocyte cultures) reactive cells, one finds that, in most strains of mice with a median life span of 2.5 years, reactivity is also quite low or non-existent by one year of age (Adler et al., 1971). This is interesting because this is still quite early in relation to the falling off in humoral immunity and in relation to the aging process (see figure 2). Therefore, we have some indication that a functional aspect of the immune system, the cell mediated-thymic dependent system, may be related to an aging process as a causative effect rather than a concurrent event. Before exploring the possible significance of the presence of an unbalanced immune system in which cellular-immune T cell function has fallen off while humoral antibody synthesis remains near normal, let us return to the autoimmune phenomena and attempt to include it in a mechanistic pathogenetic hypothesis.

Transplantation experiments have demonstrated that antigenic tissue is rejected primarily by the lymphoid cellular immune system rather than by antibody (Gowans, 1965). That is not to say that antibody can't exert a cytotoxic effect on tissue or cells, but lymphocytes appear to be the first line of defense and attack on the foreign tissue. Immuno-crippled humans or animals, either thymectomized or immune-deficient due to the non-development of the cellular immune system, or immunosuppressed with drugs or antilymphocyte serum, will maintain grafts of foreign tissue for a longer period than will normal individuals. In fact, mice which have only the humoral immune system intact can maintain transplanted human tumor tissue indefinitely (Castro, 1972). Therefore, a decrease in a cellular immune system function could have consequences which may explain the appearance of "auto" antibody and aging phenomena.

I would like to propose that the unifying event or events which could account for a decreased cellular immune function, auto-antibody, age-related disease, and aging phenomena, could be a series of viral infections. One of the important functional roles of the cellular immune system is the immunity to viral infections (Adler and Rabinowitz, 1973; Rabinowitz and Adler, 1973). Humans with decreased ability to make antibody, but with normal

cell mediated immunity, have normal clinical relationships
to viral infection. However, humans or animals with a
crippled cellular immune system may have stormy or fatal
outcomes of viral infection (Allison and Burns, 1971). One
way of relating this to the transplantation immune system
of lymphocyte function is to realize that a virus is an
intracellular parasite which, especially with RNA viruses,
at some point in the infection determines a cell surface
antigen, either an antigen directly associated with the
viral antigen, or an antigen which is a new antigen determined by the virus, but not found as part of the viral
antigen make-up (Salaman et al., 1973). Therefore, virus-
infected cells or tissue could be destroyed by lymphocytes
in an "auto" immune rejection phenomenon (Liburd et al.,
1973). The lymphocytes could in a sense destroy the virus
producing factory, thus turning off and aborting the infection. If this is the normal course of events, then what
might be the outcome of a viral infection in a cellular
immune-deficient animal or human? One might expect to find
that the virus-producing diseased tissue could continue to
produce virus and the infection could continue. The virus-
infected cells, however, would be expressing an antigen,
either viral in nature or a new antigen which would serve
to be an antigenic structure able to be recognized by antibody. Thus, the antibody could be found to be attached
to self tissue and would appear as an "auto" antibody.
But, how could the decrease in cellular immunity be explained as a result of a viral infection? There are two
possibilities that will be considered. It has been shown
that normal, non-stimulated, non-dividing lymphocytes are
very difficult to infect with virus, whereas stimulated
lymphocytes which are in mitotic cycles can be infected
with virus (Jimenez et al., 1971). Therefore, one can
hypothesize that in a viral infection the lymphocytes
which are antigen-sensitive and which attack the diseased
virus-infected tissue may themselves become vulnerable to
infection and subsequent destruction.

Another possible mechanism would be that viral-infect-
ed lymphoid tissue would acquire the capability to destroy
normal lymphoid tissue. This has been shown to happen in
mice carrying "Moloney" murine leukemia virus, in that
infected thymocytes can become cytotoxic to syngeneic un-
infected tissue (Proffitt et al., 1973). Over a period of
time and with multiple experiences with virus, it could be

expected that a decrease in cellular-lymphocyte-mediated-
immunity might occur. With the decrease in cellular
immunity one has the imbalance in the immune system and
the state where "auto" (anti cell-antigen) antibody is
present, but prolonged or chronic viral infections will
ensue. The effects of these viral infections, however,
would be crucial in the aging process. Not only would
tissue be destroyed, but viral nucleic acid genome would
be plugged into the infected cells. On a very basic examination of viral effects on normal cells, one can consider
the pronounced effects of viral infection of the diphtheria
bacillus, which then engenders production of a biologically
active protein (Pappenheimer and Gill, 1973). The results
could be cell "mutation" or carcinogenesis. If tumours
were caused, it could be that antibody in the absence of a
cell mediated rejection could actually accelerate tumour
cell growth (Shearer et al., 1973). Enzyme and hormone
patterns could be altered. Soluble antigen-antibody immune
complex disease could be initiated (Oldstone and Dixon,
1969), and all the phenomena associated with the aging
process could be a result.

It is also possible to explain the caloric restriction
and experimental hypothermic effects in prolonging life
regarding their effects on viral disease and the immune
system. We have previously shown that a deficience of a
single amino acid, arginine, can have dramatic effects on
the expression of cellular virus production and the concentration of cell membrane components (Osunkoya et al., 1970).
It would not be difficult to imagine that a caloric deficiency might have similar effects on host tissue-virus
interactions. As for low temperature effects, it is well
documented that virus cell infection and subsequent production of viral protein and nucleic acid can be affected
by temperature fluctuation. It could even be possible that
the cell-immune processes do not decrease as rapidly in
animals at low temperature or on a caloric restriction.

In summary, I would propose the following schema:
With repeated viral infections, starting possibly at
conception, the individual acquires a "library" of viral
genetic information. Concurrently, the cell-mediated
immune system undergoes a decline in activity. Viral
infected tissue that cannot be policed by the lymphocytes
is attacked by anti-viral antibody, or anti-tissue antibody
and the phenomena of auto-antibody becomes manifest. Virus

plus antibody results in immune complex disease, but not in a rejection of the diseased tissue. The infections continue causing normal tissue disease and the induction of tumours. In the absence of effective cellular immune functions the tumours are allowed to grow, maybe even encouraged to progress by anti-tumour antibody. The results of infections, decreased immune function, immune complex disease, and carcinogenesis are all included as part of the contribution of this autoimmune theory to the aging process.

REFERENCES

Adler, W. H. and Rabinowitz, S. G. (1973). J. Immunol. 110, 1354.

Adler, W. H., Takiguchi, T. and Smith, R. T. (1971). J. Immunol. 107, 1357.

Allison, A. C. and Burns, W. H. (1971). In "Immunogenicity" (F. Borek, ed.), Ch. 6, North Holland Publ. Co., Amsterdam.

Castro, J. E. (1972). Nature New Biol. 239, 83.

Giannini, D. and Sloan, R. S. (1957). Lancet 1, 525.

Gowans, J. L. (1965). Brit. Med. Bull. 21, 106.

Hallgren, H. M., Buckley, G. E. III, Gilbertsen, V. A. and Yunis, E. J. (1973). J. Immunol. 111, 1101.

Heidrick, M. L. and Makinodan, T. (1972). Gerontologia 18, 305.

Hori, Y., Perkins, E. H. and Halsall, M. K. (1973). Proc. Soc. Exp. Biol. Med. 144, 48.

Jimenez, J., Bloom, B. R., Blume, M. R. and Oettgen, H. F. (1971). J. Exp. Med. 133, 740.

Liburd, E. M., Russell, A. S. and Dossetor, J. B. (1973). J. Immunol. 111, 1288.

Makinodan, T., Heidrick, M. L. and Nordin, A. A. (1973). In "Proceedings of the Second Intern. Workshop on Primary Immunodeficiencies in Man", St. Petersburg, Fla., Feb. 1973. Sinauer Press, Stanford, Calif. (in press).

Makinodan, T. and Peterson, W. J. (1964). J. Immunol. 93, 886.

Oldstone, M. B. A. and Dixon, F. J. (1969). J. Exp. Med. 129, 483.

Osunkoya, B. O., Adler, W. H. and Smith, R. T. (1970). Nature 227, 398.

Pappenheimer, A. M. and Gill, D. M. (1973). _Science_ 182, 353.

Parish, C. R. and Liew, F. Y. (1972). _J. Exp. Med._ 135, 298.

Peavy, D. L., Adler, W. H., Shands, J. W. and Smith, R. T. (1974). _J. Immunol._ (in press).

Proffitt, M. R., Hirsch, M. S. and Black, P. H. (1973). _Science_ 182, 821.

Rabinowitz, S. G. and Adler, W. H. (1973). _J. Immunol._ 110, 1345.

Salaman, M. H., Turk, J. L. and Wedderburn, N. (1973). _Transplantation_ 16, 585.

Shearer, W. T., Philpott, G. W. and Parker, C. W. (1973). _Science_ 182, 1357.

Takiguchi, T., Adler, W. H. and Smith, R. T. (1971). _J. Exp. Med._ 133, 63.

Thomsen, O. and Kettel, K. (1929). _Z. Immunitätsforsch._ 63, 67.

Waldorf, D. S., Wilkens, R. F. and Decker, J. C. (1968). _J. Am. Med. Assoc._ 203, 111.

Walford, R. L. (1969). "Immunologic Theory of Aging." Ch. IV, Munksgaard, Copenhagen.

CROSSLINKAGE AND THE AGING PROCESS

Johan Bjorksten

Bjorksten Research Foundation
Madison, Wisconsin 53701

Of all chemical reactions, crosslinkage is the one by
which the smallest amount of interference can produce the
greatest amount of damage. Inasmuch as components for
these reactions are plentifully available in all living
cells and the time available for the reactions to take
place is from 70 to 110 years in man, it is certain that
these reactions will take place with obvious and unavoidable consequences.

Evidence of crosslinkage as a principal causative reaction in aging has been summarized before (Bjorksten,
1971). Two illustrative examples will be given, however,
as follows:

1. Crosslinkage of DNA

Figure 1 shows a part of a DNA helix and a crosslinking agent, typified by a small molecule with a chemically active site on each end. One end attaches itself to
the DNA helix engaging one strand only. The body's defense
mechanism cannot loosen the linkage, but it can and does
cut out a piece of the strand including the crosslinker.
This is excreted (figure 1a) and the DNA strand is repaired
using the remaining untouched strand as the template.

However, in a small number of instances, the repair
mechanism is not rapid enough. Figure 2 shows what happens
if the crosslinker, while still attached to the DNA strand,
connects with its other end to the corresponding site on
the other DNA strand. If the defense mechanism excises the
supplementary corresponding segments on two strands (figure
2a), no template will remain for the repair. The damage is
then irreparable (Howard-Flanders and Boyce, 1966).   On
the other hand, if the defense mechanism fails to act

43

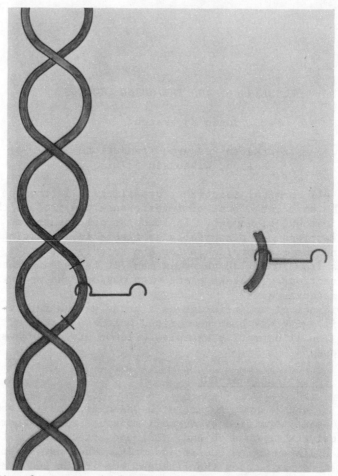

Fig. 1 A crosslinking agent attaches itself at one
point of a DNA molecule, involving one strand only. Right,
the agent is excised by defense mechanisms together with a
piece of the DNA affected. The damage is then repaired, the
unaffected strand being the template.

altogether (figure 2b), the crosslinkage remains in position. In the next cell division, the DNA strands will
start parting normally, and each of them will start synthesizing its complement, so as to produce two complete

new DNA molecules, from two single strands. When this
process reaches the irreparable crosslinkage between the
two strands, the parting can no longer proceed, nor can
the construction of the two strands up to that point be
undone. The result is a Y-shaped monstrosity which is not
viable, and the cell dies or possibly sometimes is able to
mutate.

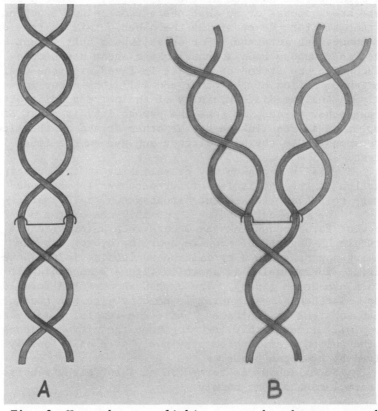

Fig. 2 Here the crosslinking agent has become attached to the second strand of DNA before the defense mechanism
could excise it. When this has happened the cell is doomed.
If the crosslinker is excised, there will be no template
for repair as both strands are involved at the same point.
If the crosslinker remains, it will block the normal parting of strands in mitosis at a stage where the resultant
DNA can neither return to normal nor complete the division.

At this point, it seems appropriate to emphasize the reason why crosslinking agents, which are all at least bifunctional, have a vastly greater efficiency in disturbing DNA function than do their monofunctional analogues (Haddow et al., 1948; Alexander and Connell, 1962).

The statement was made by a previous speaker that the probability is extremely small that both strands of DNA might become damaged at the same site, so that a complete break occurs or so that one strand cannot function as template for the repair of the other. This is true only for monovalent mutagens. For crosslinkers this is not at all true, because once a crosslinking agent has become attached to one strand of DNA, it is fixed with one end. The random motion of the other end will thus occur incessantly in the immediate vicinity of the corresponding site of the other strand, so that the probability is great of completing a crosslinkage to the other strand at the site corresponding to the site already engaged on the first strand.

This is a reason why crosslinking is the principal reaction in the initiation of irreparable "spontaneous" damage to DNA and consequent "spontaneous" cell death.

The simplest, and very possibly one of the more frequent fatal crosslinkages occurs when a formaldehyde molecule, CH_2O, gets in anywhere near the hydrogen bonds linking a purine- to a pyrimidine-nucleoside in the base-pairing, for example, as shown in figure 3 according to Watson and Crick (1953). The oxygen atom of the formaldehyde will then almost instantly combine with the two active hydrogen atoms as indicated, while the remaining methylene group will irreversibly lock together the nitrogen atoms of the paired bases, which previously were only loosely united by hydrogen bonds.

Formaldehyde is formed in at least eight reactions in normal metabolism, namely:

1. Dimethylglycine + $1/2$ O_2 $\longrightarrow$ Sarcosine + formaldehyde

2. Sarcosine + FAD $\longrightarrow$ glycine + formaldehyde + $FADH_2$

3. N-methyl-1-amino acids + O_2 $\longrightarrow$ 1-amino acids + formaldehyde

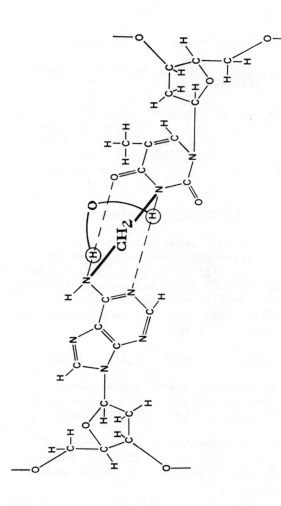

Fig. 3 A segment of a DNA molecule (according to Watson and Crick, 1953). Two nucleosides are normally tied together by hydrogen bonds as shown (i.e., dotted lines). The two strands thus connected by a very large number of similarly paired purines and pyrimidines continue vertically on both sides of the figure. A migrant molecule of formaldehyde (CH_2O) (center, heavy type) has accidentally come into the proximity of the hydrogen bonds; its oxygen has reacted with the hydrogens to form H_2O, while its $CH_2=$ group has established a methylene bridge between purine and pyrimidine, as a strong covalent bond. The reaction is strongly exothermic (+217.6 kcal/mole) and virtually instantaneous.

47

4. Erythrulose-1-phosphate $\longrightarrow$ dihydroxyacetone phosphate + formaldehyde

5. D-ribose-5-phosphate $\longrightarrow$ erythrulose-1-PO_4 + formaldehyde

6. Alpha-keto-gamma-hydroxybutyrate $\longrightarrow$ pyruvate + formaldehyde

7. Serine + aldolase $\longrightarrow$ glycine + formaldehyde

8. Deoxycytidylate + formaldehyde $\longrightarrow$ 5-hydroxy-methyldeoxycytidylate

The alkylating type of crosslinking agents for DNA have been discussed in some detail by Alexander and Lett (1960). Many additional crosslinking agents have been discussed in connection with aging (Bjorksten, 1971). Almost any of these could take the place of formaldehyde in the above example.

2. Crosslinkage of nongenetic macromolecules

In spite of the obvious importance and the proven sensitivity of DNA to crosslinkage, DNA may not be the most important factor. In a lifetime, crosslinkages will form between all other types of large molecules, wherever one of the billions of crosslinker molecules present in the organism accidentally locks onto a large molecule. The result is shown in figure 4.

Steps Toward Application of the Crosslinking Theory

Crosslinking of proteins is indeed a most serious problem, since the amorphous deposits, such as hyalin and amyloid, which accumulate in the body with aging are largely proteinaceous.

When a physician is 99% certain of a diagnosis of pneumonia, he treats for pneumonia. He does not wait for the autopsy to be 100% certain of the correctness of his diagnosis before doing anything.

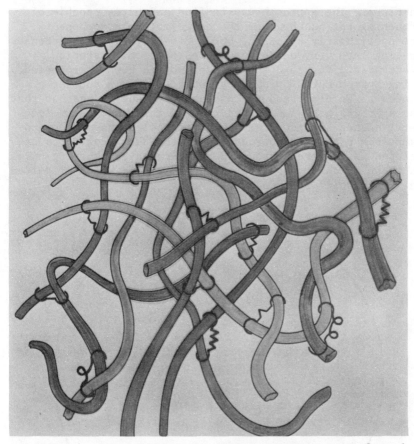

Fig. 4 Over a lifetime, dense aggregates are formed intracellularly, by random accidental crosslinkage of any available large molecules with any available crosslinking agents. These aggregates are too dense to be touched by available enzymes. As they accumulate, they may contribute to age-dependent deterioration even more than the genetic molecules.

We were sufficiently certain of having a sound base, to proceed toward practical application. Clearly, the very large number of possible crosslinkers (Bjorksten, 1963, 1971) makes it pointless to try to attack these specifically, either preventively or when already locked

in place. The approach was to find an enzyme capable of
attacking the backbone of the large molecule components,
not particularly specific, but above all, capable of penetrating into very dense structures overcoming steric
hindrances. Figure 5 shows in principle how we proceeded,
using a procedure employed by Dubos (1945) in another
context. We dispersed an insoluble residue in agar so that
the agar was grey and turbid, poured this suspension into
Petri dishes and inoculated with miscellaneous microorganisms from plausible sources. Here and there, cultures developed which were surrounded by clear halos: the organisms
in these colonies were secreting exoenzymes which dissolved
the "insoluble" residue.

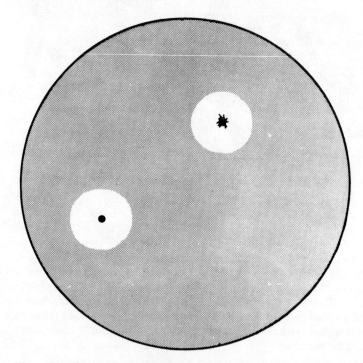

Fig. 5 The dense structures of figure 4 were isolated
from old human brain, pulverized and dispersed in agar,
rendering the agar grey. A suspension of mixed soil organisms was used as inoculum. Two colonies have developed
clear halos, showing that these colonies excrete enzymes
capable of dissolving the dispersed "gerogenic" aggregates.

Briefly, in six years we have isolated about 140 such cultures. Significantly, the majority of these were strains of one organism, Bacillus cereus. There are many others as well. We have isolated enzymes from these organisms (Bjorksten et al., 1971a; Schenk and Bjorksten, 1973), a few of which enzymes were effective in dissolving cross-linked preparations in vitro. The key to their efficiency seems to be that, like insulin, they are oligomer systems in equilibrium, so that a certain low percentage is a monomer of very low molecular weight, perhaps as low as 1,500. Such small monomers can penetrate where the larger oligomers cannot. One of these enzymes in particular was found to be effective in vitro (Bjorksten et al., 1972) in rapidly dissolving hyalin deposits from autopsy sections from kidney of a human, dead from hypertensive disease.

The enzyme is active at pH 7.0. It dissolves not only the hyalin, but also surrounding tissues. This is not important, because the dosage can be modulated to stay low enough so that the normal tissue has time to be replaced faster than it is catabolized, while the crosslinked hyalin is not being replaced at any similar rate.

In order to test for toxicity, we injected intraperitoneally in 10-month-old mice 100 or 200 Congocoll units (Nelson et al., 1961)*.

When nothing untoward happened, we continued these injections once a month with two animals each for two levels of enzyme concentrations and two controls. The animals are now 19 months old. One of the controls is dead, while the other is greyer, slower and fatter than the animals which have received the injections. The animal which has received the greatest amount of enzyme is the least grey and weighs less than the control. This was not true at the beginning of the experiment.

Of course, it is impossible to form any firm conclusion from these few animals in a test originally intended only to check for toxicity, but the results are not discouraging. We have detected no chronic toxicity or immun-

---

*Congocoll assays were run by a modification of the method of Nelson, et al. (1961) using 20 mg of Congocoll in 1.0 ml of 0.1 M Tris buffer (pH 7.2) containing 10^{-4} M $CaCl_2$ for 30 minutes at 30°C. Following 10 seconds shaking, each sample was diluted with 5 ml of the Tris buffer and light transmission measured.

ological reaction. On the contrary, the results appear to
be quite beneficial to the treated animals.

In order to facilitate further work, we have enterically coated the enzyme granules and made possible oral
administration. The enzyme is quite stable above pH 6.0,
but below pH 5.0 it is rapidly inactivated and so must be
protected from the low pH of the stomach. The coated
granules are readily eaten by mice.

Like other workers, we have found protease inhibitors
in the blood. The enzyme appears to be at least partially
bound to these materials. Work to date clearly indicates
that a significant amount of enzyme reaches the blood of
those mice which have eaten the enterically coated enzyme
granules.

Figure 6 shows the color due to the dissolution of the
blood cells separated by centrifugation from blood from one
mouse which received the enzyme orally for two weeks, and
a control. This test, repeated many times, can be variously interpreted, but in any case illustrates the difference
which exists between the blood of the control mouse and
that of the mouse which was orally administered the enzyme
in question.

This is where we stand. The next step should be to
prepare at least one large fermenter batch of the enzyme.
On the basis of numerous runs in 14,000 ml Brunswick fer-
menters, we anticipate that 400 gallons of broth should
give us about 5,000 grams of enzyme, precipitated and
purified on two columns to activity of about 150,000 Congocoll units per gram. With this, we could supply material
to anyone who wants to experiment with it.

Concurrently, we shall refine and streamline the production methods for at least seven enzymes of the same
general character, prepared from other organisms. At least
three of those we have selected are even more filterable
through ultrafilters than is the B. cereus enzyme, indicating still better penetrating properties. It would indeed
be extremely lucky for us if the very first enzyme selected
from 140 colonies should meet every possible requirement;
instead, we must be prepared for a lengthy and laborious
search. However, the path we have taken is solidly founded
and, we believe, should be followed to a conclusion.

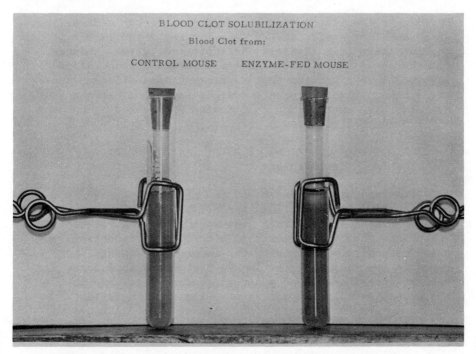

Fig. 6 Rate of blood clot lysis. The right tube contains blood solubilized from the clot of an enzyme-consuming mouse. The left tube contains blood solubilized from the clot of a mouse receiving no added enzyme.

Comments on the Relation of Crosslinkage Theory to Other Principal Theories of Aging

An evaluation of the crosslinkage theory in the light of established criteria has been presented earlier (Bjorksten, 1971). In view of subsequent developments, the following, more specific comments appear timely:

The cell death theory

The cell death theory and the crosslinkage theory are mutually consistent. Hayflick (1965) has advanced compelling evidence that cell death after a certain number of divisions is a principal factor of senility and death.

Hayflick's conclusion that the principal factor controlling
aging does not reside in DNA (see figures 2 and 3) but in
the cytoplasm (see figure 4) is supported by the findings
(Bjorksten et al., 1971b) that much more RNA than DNA is
involved in the tritium traced "frozen" metabolites. The
crosslinkage theory presents a mechanism which explains
how otherwise unexplained cell deaths are caused by phenomena inherent in the growth process, but hopefully not irreversible.

The immunologic theory

The immunologic theory and the crosslinkage theory
are mutually consistent. Walford (1969) has advanced compelling evidence, confirmed and expended by many other
scientists that autoimmunity is a critically important
aging mechanism. Underlying the immunologic theory, however, is the fact that the immune response deteriorates
with aging. There is no apparent reason to believe that
the cause for this age-dependent deterioration of the
immune system is different from that of other glandular
and cellular systems and of the "spontaneous cell death",
namely, the effect of random uncontrolled crosslinkages in:

a. Creating pervasive crosslinked cages or network
impeding intracellular transport and thereby disturbing
the various functions of the immune system. This type of
obstruction and its genesis have already been discussed
(figure 4).

b. Causing crosslinkages involving essential molecules
thus hampering their function.

c. Causing destruction of sites in DNA which govern
immunologic functions (as shown in figure 2).

A penetrating study of these aspects would seem to be
indicated.

I shall take this opportunity to answer a few
questions raised by Dr. Walford in his comprehensive book
"The Immune Theory of Aging" (1969).

1. How can the crosslinkage theory explain the fact

54

that enormously larger doses of X-ray are required to produce life shortening in insects than in vertebrates?

The insects appear to age by processes largely
different from those of the vertebrates. In any event,
the time spans for reaction differ so greatly, that it is
difficult to assume a direct analogy without further study.

2. Why are mice on the day of their birth much more
susceptible to the life shortening effects of low dosage
irradiation than when they are a few days old?

After a few days the number of cells will have
multiplied with the concomitant increase in the reserves
and replacement possibilities of critical molecules.

3. Why is it that in Campanularia, a marine hydroid,
doses as enormous as 200,000 r may actually increase life
span?

The marine hydroids have an extremely low solids
content. They may consist of up to 97% water. They are
transparent to light and much more so to X-rays, which in
the main pass through them ineffectually. Finally, the
relatively low oxygen content in the aquatic environment
may greatly mitigate the crosslinking effect of radiation.

I can readily understand that it is natural for an
immunologist or geneticist to be struck by some similari-
ties of radiation effects with aging. However, as every
polymer chemist knows, ionizing radiation has at least two
principal effects: fission of molecules and crosslinkage.
Thus, the analogy between time-dependent aging and radiation is, at best, only partial. A further complication is
the oxygen dependence of radiation. From a chemist's
standpoint, these facts seemed so obvious that I failed to
elaborate on them as, in the light of Dr. Walford's comments (p. 201), I should have done. Regarding the infer-
ences of Walford on that page, it should be clear from the
discussion in connection with figures 1 - 3 above that I
do not consider crosslinking as a mainly post-mitotic
phenomenon. Alexander (1962) elucidates this point further.
The life span is far less dependent on the rate of crosslinking than on the rate and efficiency of the repair of
macromolecules before an incipient crosslinkage has become
completed, and on steric hindrances for enzyme action established. Crosslinking and repair versus dilution and

55

excretion go on incessantly. It is the ratio between these processes which largely governs life spans.

The free radical theory

The free radical theory is a special case of the crosslinkage theory, in which the crosslinking agents involved are free radicals. That crosslinking agents as such are involved in aging was stated by Bjorksten (1941, 1942). That free radicals are crosslinkage agents was pointed out in the polymer field by Charlesby (1953). Harman (1956) stressed the role of free radicals in aging.

The nature of the fatty acid oxidation effects is still in question. It has long been known that proteins are crosslinked[*] in the presence of oxidizing unsaturated fatty acids or glycerides. Isaacs (1915) mentions this as already then well known as a means for attaching gelatin compounds to oiled paper or cloth backings; the art of soft leather tanning used this tanning reaction even earlier. Fahrion (1891) stated that the oxidation of oil is essential for tanning (crosslinking) action and recommended the Mackey test for spontaneous oxidation of oils to evaluate the oils for tanning of chamois leather. Procter (1904) assumed acrolein to be the principal factor in tanning by oil oxidation. Over 20 years ago, Bjorksten (1941) emphasized the connection between natural aging and the then extensive knowledge existing on crosslinkages in the leather, photographic film and hectograph fields.

The effect of oxidizing oil in reacting with large molecules has been variously attributed to the formation of peroxides, aldehydes, and free radicals (Fahrion, 1891, 1903; Procter, 1904; Gustavson, 1956). All of these are evidently present to a more or less pronounced degree. Perhaps the aldehydes are the most active of these crosslinking components. On the basis of odor alone, Procter (1904) attributed to acrolein the principal effect in tanning. Bjorksten (1941, 1942) based his initial entry in the aging field on observations ascribed to aldehydes formed by oxidation of linseed oil in the presence of proteins. Küntzel and Nungesser (1951) stated that tanning with aldehydes could give leather similar to that obtained with oxidizing oil, and that aldehyde in the presence of

---

[*]The word "tanned" is used for crosslinking in the earlier technical literature.

oil caused tanning under conditions precluding the oxidation of the oil.

Bjorksten and Collbring (1964) showed that when a
gelatin gel containing 0.17% unsaturated fatty acid is ir-
radiated with ultraviolet light for 3 hours and then
placed in the dark, the melting point increase caused by
crosslinkage mounts steadily (in the dark) for several
weeks, until the gel decomposes before it melts. Such
stability is usually not attributed to free radicals,
although it is known to occur at times. A similar melting
point increase can be obtained by adding one of the lower
aldehydes to the gelatin gel, omitting the radiation and
the unsaturated fat.

Regardless of whether the effect of oxidizing oil on
protein is due to aldehydes or to free radicals or peroxides or as seems most probable, to all of these, it should
be helpful to use antioxidants to control the random oxidation processes. This was already pointed out by Hickman
in 1935 and used as a point in merchandising vitamin E by
Distillation Products Industries. In particular, it seems
to indicate a liberal intake of tocopherol or equivalent
when the diet is high in unsaturated lipids of any kind.
Since the free radical effects represent only a relatively
small part of the total crosslinking influences present
during a lifetime, countering them cannot be expected to
have extremely spectacular effects. This is confirmed by
tests to date (Witting, 1972).

In a recent paper by Tappel, et al. (1973), figure 6
shows that free radical quenching antioxidants in large
excess of what was given to the control animals in a good
laboratory diet did not increase overall life span, but,
on the contrary, seemed to shorten it somewhat.

Somatic mutations

The theory of somatic mutations as causative in aging
was shaken when, in 1948, Haddow, et al. showed that the
tumor-growth inhibiting activity of the nitrogen mustards
was confined to polyfunctional compounds only and that
bifunctional compounds were 50 times more active than their
monofunctional analogues in the production of chromosome
breaks.

Alexander and Connell (1962) showed that, in mice,
two bifunctional mutagens, or alternatively 1100 r of

X-rays reduced the life span by about 1/3, while a monovalent mutagen of similar mutagenic potency had no corresponding effect. This, taken in conjunction with Haddow's
observation, should suffice to dispose of any theory which
ascribes to somatic mutations any key role in aging.

The stability of DNA is great; it is stable for many
months in solution. Even if it is, on occasion, present
in a more sensitive single strand state, its stability is
thousands of times higher than if a crosslinking agent is
added. In that case, it can be crosslinked and precipitated in seconds. It seems far fetched indeed to think in
terms of spontaneous instability when crosslinking agents
are demonstrably present and extremely active on DNA.

The persistence of theories which have been disproven
many years ago is regrettable, as it causes dispersion of
research efforts into inherently fruitless channels.

Conclusion

The crosslinkage theory meets all of the criteria
established for the evaluation of aging theories. As for
molecular data, molecules have been found in old tissue
which comprise typical components of DNA, RNA and peptides,
respectively covalently bound together (Bjorksten et al.,
1971b; Acharya et al., 1972). This is consistent with
figure 5, above.

The crosslinking theory offers a clear path for
attack on age-dependent deterioration. This, vigorously
pursued, should lead to a truly dramatic extension of the
vigorous part of life, and to the control of senility and
degenerative disease.

References

Acharya, P. V. N., Ashman, S. M. and Bjorksten, J. (1972).
Finska Kemistsamfundets Medd. 81, 70.
Alexander, P. (1962). In "The Effects of Ionizing Radia-
tions on Immune Processes" (C. A. Leone, ed.), pp. 75-
98, Gordon and Breach Sc. Publishers, New York.
Alexander, P. and Connell, D. I. (1962). In "UNESCO
Symposium on Cellular Basis and Aetiology of Late
Somatic Effect of Ionizing Radiation" (R.J.C. Harris,
ed.), pp. 259-265, Academic Press, New York.
Alexander, P. and Lett, J. T. (1960). Biochem. Pharmacol.

4, 34.
Bjorksten, J. (1941). Chem. Ind. U.S.A. 48, 746.
Bjorksten, J. (1942). Chem. Ind. U.S.A. 50, 69.
Bjorksten, J. (1963). Gerontologia 8, 182.
Bjorksten, J. (1971). Finska Kemistsamfundets Medd. 80, 23.
Bjorksten, J., Acharya, P. V. N., Ashman, S. M. and
  Wetlaufer, D. B. (1971b). J. Am. Geriat. Soc. 19, 572.
Bjorksten, J., Bloodworth, J. M. B., Jr. and Buetow, R.
  (1972). J. Am. Geriat. Soc. 20, 148.
Bjorksten, J. and Collbring, T. (1964). Proc. Sci. Sect.
  Toilet Goods Assoc. 42, 1.
Bjorksten, J., Weyer, E. R. and Ashman, S. M. (1971a).
  Finska Kemistsamfundets Medd. 80, 70.
Charlesby, A. (1953). Plastics (London) 18, 70, 142.
Dubos, R. (1945). "The Bacterial Cell." Harvard University
  Press, Cambridge, Mass.
Fahrion, W. (1891). Z. Angew. Chem. 4, 172, 446, 691.
Fahrion, W. (1903). Z. Angew. Chem. 16, 665.
Gustavson, K. H. (1956). "The Chemistry of Tanning
  Processes." Academic Press, New York.
Haddow, A., Kon, G. A. R. and Ross, W. C. J. (1948).
  Nature 162, 824.
Harman, D. (1956). J. Gerontol. 11, 298.
Hayflick, L. (1965). Exp. Cell Res. 37, 614.
Hickman, K. C. D. (1935). Personal communication.
Howard-Flanders, P. and Boyce, R. P. (1966). Radiation Res.
  Suppl. 6, 156.
Isaacs, A. (1915). U. S. Patent 1,151,951.
Küntzel, A. and Nungesser, T. (1951). Das Leder 2, 233.
Nelson, W. L., Ciaccio, E. I. and Hess, G. P. (1961). Anal.
  Biochem. 2, 39.
Procter, H. R. (1904). "Principles of Leather Manufacture."
  Spon, London.
Schenk, R. U. and Bjorksten, J. (1973). Finska Kemistsam-
  fundets Medd. 82, 26.
Tappel, A., Fletcher, B. and Deamer, D. (1973). J. Gerontol.
  28, 415.
Walford, R. (1969). "The Immunologic Theory of Aging."
  Williams & Wilkins, Baltimore.
Watson, J. D. and Crick, F. H. C. (1953). Nature 171, 737.
Witting, L. A. (1972). Ann. N. Y. Acad. Sci. 203, 192.

FREE RADICALS AND THE AGING PROCESS

Paul Gordon

Department of Physiology
Northwestern University School of Medicine

INTRODUCTION

Free radicals are highly reactive cellular components derived from atoms or molecules in which an electron pair has been transiently separated into two electrons that exhibit independence of motion (Pryor, 1973). Because the magnetic moments of these electrons are no longer complementary, such radicals exhibit a large increment of free energy and will oxidatively attack adjacent molecules, especially if these molecules are partially activated (Demopoulos, 1973a). In organic systems, this can result in the extraction of α-methylenyl hydrogens, as well as other activated atoms, from lipids (Tappel, 1973), nucleic acids (Myers, 1973), and other species. Free radicals can be demonstrated to occur spontaneously in vitro and in vivo by spectroscopic methods that detect the appropriate electron spin changes (Commoner et al., 1957; Harman and Piette, 1966; Ingram, 1958). The occurrence of free radicals, furthermore, has been reported to increase in certain pathological conditions in vivo, as when normal breast tissue becomes neoplastic in humans (Wallace et al., 1970).

In biological systems, the molecule that most commonly generates free radicals is oxygen (Demopoulos, 1973a). It normally does so during the course of physiological oxidative processes that occur in the oxidation chain of mitochondrial cristae (Commoner et al., 1957). Oxygen also generates free radicals in vitro, during the course of

random events in which molecular changes occur that are destructive and profound, and which result from serial oxidations in organic structures rich in unsaturated lipids
(Tappel, 1965). Prime among vulnerable structures are mitochondrial and microsomal membranes (Di Luzio, 1973; Wills,
1970). These membranes contain enzymes, such as monoamine
oxidase and microsome cytochrome oxidase, whose normal
function is to catalyze oxidations via molecular oxygen.
Through membrane destabilization, such oxygen-utilizing
systems can deteriorate and, as a result, local lipid
structures, rather than normal substrate, can become the
subject of oxidation (Demopoulos, 1973b; Packer et al.,
1967).

Because the activated states represented by free
radicals can result in molecular pathology, when they are
generated external to normally functioning oxidase systems,
free radical formation and oxidative activity have been
proposed as generative of specific pathological states in
vivo. On the basis of experimental evidence, such pathology has been proposed as germane to irradiation injury, to
lung pathology induced by the gaseous oxidative pollutants
SO_2, NO_2, and O_3 (Demopoulos, 1973b; Goldstein et al.,
1969), to carbon tetrachloride and ethanol injury to the
liver (Di Luzio, 1973), and, of particular relevance to
this chapter, to biological aging (Harman, 1956, 1961,
1962).

Where aging is concerned, the view has been advanced
that free radical-induced alterations of significant molecules create sites of randomness and malfunction that
accumulate during the life span (Harman, 1956), either in
the nucleus (presumably in genes, as somatic mutations)
(Brooks et al., 1973; Medvedev, 1964) or in the cytoplasm
(as alterations of significant membrane surfaces and control molecules) (Packer et al., 1967). Implicit in the
concept of the accumulation of faulty molecules and cellular debris is an inadequacy in function of nuclear and
cytoplasmic repair mechanisms that recognize aberrant
molecules and eliminate them by repair, catabolism, or
extrusion.

Although chromosomal aberrations do accumulate with
aging, probably as a result of free radical attack, the
effect of such events on cellular functioning would appear
to be blunted by genic redundancy. Recent data discussed
by Drs. Hayflick and Sinex in other chapters of this

volume suggest that the major functional changes that develop in cells with aging occur, in fact, not in the nucleus, but in the cytoplasm. These findings permit us to restrict our examination to literature concerned with cytoplasmic events.

FREE RADICALS AND LIPID PEROXIDATION: CURRENT STATUS

An increasing number of workers are publishing data which support the view that free radical-induced peroxidation of unsaturated fatty acids in organelle membranes and surfaces in vivo is a major determinant of biological aging. This point of view is by no means uncontested.

Let us first consider areas of universal agreement. Agreement is general that free radical formation produces peroxidative damage in diverse biological preparations in vitro (Barber and Bernheim, 1967; Green, 1972; Tappel, 1973; Wills, 1970); that molecular oxygen plays an important role in the chain of events that generates this pathology (Demopoulos, 1973a; Pryor, 1973); that transitional metals (such as tungstate, copper or iron salts) play an important permissive role in such peroxidizing systems (Demopoulos, 1973a, b), as they may lower, by as much as five orders of magnitude, the energy of activation for lipid peroxide formation. Also, there is general agreement that tocopherols, ascorbic acid, glutathione, and other chemically unrelated antioxidants contribute to an antioxidant potential in body fluids and tissues that can oppose the peroxidation of cell structures under discussion, at least in vitro (Di Luzio, 1973; Green, 1972; Harman, 1962; Milvy, 1973; Tappel, 1972).

The area of current controversy concerns the assigning of relative significance to specific in vivo experiments and, of course, to the conclusion of some that, despite striking in vitro findings, there is no good evidence for free radical action on unsaturated lipids and other substrates in the living state (Bunyan et al., 1969; Green, 1972; Lucy, 1972).

Although the full importance of free radical-induced pathology to biological aging is far from determined, one can conclude from the experimental evidence that free radical formation and free radical induction of pathology in vivo are real events in aging and in other states. This

63

is true even if one considers experiments that fail to identify lipid peroxides _in vivo_ in vitamin E-deficient rats. Although these studies are referred to by Green (1972) as a refutation of the significance of free radical-induced peroxidative injury to the _in vivo_ situation, it would appear that the failure to find significant levels of lipid peroxides by direct chemical tissue analysis in a particular disease state does not eliminate their possible contribution to this disease state or other states. This is so because of the limited metastability of lipid peroxides, i.e. their great tendency to progress through chain reactions beyond the active forms to end products (Gutman, 1970; Pryor, 1973; Tappel, 1965, 1972).

In the light of other positive data, the view of Green (1972) need have even less relevance to aging, in which such destructive processes as free radical-induced lipid peroxidations can be viewed as occurring with relatively low frequency. Here, end-products of reactions accumulate in non-dividing cells over the life span, until significant boundary conditions of functional loss are reached.

LIPID PEROXIDATION _IN VIVO_: NEW EVIDENCE

It is most significant to the _in vivo_ lipid peroxidation hypothesis that Di Luzio (1973) has demonstrated the presence of conjugated dienes, a class of lipid peroxidation products in the phospholipid fraction of fresh human plasma. Conjugated diene ultraviolet absorbance was not found in fresh animal serum, was found in oils rich in polyunsaturated fatty acids, but not in oils poor in these fatty acids; and, most important, was reduced in humans by adding additional vitamin E to, and was enhanced by removing vitamin E from the diet. Finally, the change in concentration of conjugated diene was related by Di Luzio (1973) to parallel change in the lipid soluble antioxidant activity of plasma.

There are a number of other direct lines of experimental evidence for the occurrence of damaging lipid peroxidations _in vivo_ which I find convincing. Histological and biochemical studies have characterized lipofuscin pigments which accumulate in animal tissues during the life span (Reichel et al., 1968; Strehler, 1964). The composition of these pigments indicates that they result from the

peroxidation of polyunsaturated lipids and their crosslinking with proteins in subcellular membranes. On the
other hand, there have been direct measurements from tissue
specimens of products of vitamin E formed, which indicate
that vitamin E in the normal animal is involved in stopping
the chain reaction of lipid peroxidation in vivo (Tappel,
1965, 1972). In other words, vitamin E has been success-
fully replaced in the animal diet by structurally dissimilar lipid soluble antioxidants, suggesting again that the
physiological role of vitamin E in vivo is, at least in
part, to serve an antioxidant function and suppress lipid
peroxidation (Bieri and Anderson, 1960; Harman, 1961;
Tappel, 1973; Tappel et al., 1973).

Important new support for the significance of lipid
peroxidation as an in vivo event is to be found in the work
of Tappel and coworkers (1973), who demonstrated the presence of a chloroform-methanol extractable fluorescent substance in testis, heart and brain, that is identical to the
fluorescence of a product of the chain reaction of lipid
peroxidation, malondialdehyde, when cross-linked with amino
acids or proteins. This fluorescent fat derivative, obviously a class of lipofuscin or age pigment, increased with
aging in these three organs; and, most important, this
increase with age was found to be significantly inhibited
in testis and heart by the addition of an antioxidant and
nutrient mixture to the normal basal diet. The additive
mixture included DL-α-tocopherol acetate, butylated hydroxytoluene, ascorbic acid, DL-methionine and sodium selenite
(Tappel et al., 1973).

At least one investigator proposes that the antioxidant protection afforded by vitamin E is not directly related to its antioxidative properties, but rather to
stereochemical properties which specifically allow it to
be intercalated into the structure of membranes containing
certain common classes of polyunsaturated lipids. In these
membranes, vitamin E is shown to play a condensing and
stabilizing role (Lucy, 1972). In my opinion, the observations that lead to this conclusion provide a second contribution that vitamin E may make to the prevention of
lipid peroxidative damage in tissues, but they do not in-
validate the evidence for direct antioxidative activity.

A REVIEW OF THE POTENTIALS FOR
FREE RADICAL-INDUCED PATHOLOGY IN VIVO

Recent published reviews (Barber and Bernheim, 1967) and symposia (Demopoulos, 1973c; Nair and Kayden, 1972) allow the reader to gain an extensive overview of the evolution of concepts concerning pathology provoked by free radical formation in tissues and, as well, the possible involvement of such pathology in the aging process. In this discussion, we will, therefore, only briefly review the chemical events that are involved in free radical-induced tissue damage and devote more space to areas that are now or will be, we think, at the periphery of knowledge and subjects of controversy.

As indicated, prime among the targets of free radical pathology are biological membranes rich in unsaturated lipids. These include membranes of organelles, such as mitochondria, microsomes, and, to a lesser degree, free ribosomes and the cell surface. When free radicals form, the chemical and structural changes that are produced are progressive in many instances, because of the potential for free radicals to generate other free radicals in the manner of a chain reaction, and because of the limited, but real metastability of certain lipid-free radicals or free radical-produced reactive intermediates within biological membranes. Since molecular oxygen will form free radicals under the appropriate conditions and since the free energy required to form free radicals is greatly reduced, in turn, by transitional metals common to cells, such as iron or copper in both organic and inorganic salt forms, conditions in metabolizing cells would seem to be permissive for free radical formation in domains containing iron or copper protein, as mitochondria or microsomes.

One quality that characterizes free radical action is that, apart from contributions in oxidase action that have been specified, free radicals do not appear to contain or reflect any useful biological information. Their actions on membranes, therefore, represent the replacement of genetically determined order by randomness.

In the introduction of a recent article examining the spontaneous and irradiation-induced lipid peroxidation of microsomal membranes in the presence of molecular oxygen, Wills (1970) suggests that there may be some extramitochondrial biofeedback role to this apparently universal

oxidative process in cytoplasm. However, he fails to
expand on this point, underscoring instead the extensive-
ness of microsomal deterioration that was produced.

This leads to a point deserving emphasis, viz., in
addition to being apparently randomly distributed across
vulnerable locations, the damage that is produced by free
radical formation in vitro can be locally catastrophic.
This results from oxidizing chain reactions which produce
both cross-linking and splitting of lipid chains, the
cross-linking of lipids with proteins and the generation
of anomalous carboxylate groups that then comprise points
of hydrophobic loss, or anionic tunnels, which would make
for a leaky altered membrane (Demopoulos, 1973a; Seligman
and Demopoulos, 1973; Tappel, 1973). That these events
can and do occur in model systems in vitro is well documented. The evidence for their spontaneous occurrence in
the living organism during aging will now be considered.

EVIDENCE FOR THE SPONTANEOUS OCCURRENCE OF
FREE RADICAL-INDUCED PATHOLOGY IN AGING

Accumulation of lipid peroxidation injury of biological membranes in vivo during aging should produce:

1) cells with an altered permeability to electro-
   lytes.

2) microsomes and mitochondria which have a
   greater degree of heterogeneity in function
   and structure.

3) microsomes deficient in cholesterol. As a
   result of disorganization and a reduction
   of lipid polyunsaturation, microsomes lose
   affinity for cholesterol, which sterol is
   known to have more stringent steric requirements than olefins and to locate preferen-
   tially at points of unsaturation in lipid
   aliphatic domains.

4) microsomes that, in their heterogeneity,
   exhibit domains of increased hydrophobic,
   as well as increased hydrophilic behavior.
   Thus, as a result of lipid peroxidation

67

phenomena, where points of unsaturation are extinguished by aliphatic addition phenomena and cross-chain linking, hydrophilicity will be reduced; whereas, if these events proceed to chain breaking and the formation of carboxyl groups, hydrophilicity will be increased.

5) biochemical events that depend on appropriate genetically determined relations between enzymes and contiguous membrane structures, as would be the case for:

a) enzyme activities located within membranes or exogenous enzymes attacking components of membranes,

b) facilitated transport processes across membranes, and

c) hormone-receptor interactions in membranes.

6) an accumulation of products of lipid peroxidation within cells and in body fluids, such as the bloodstream.

7) a suppression of these changes by the addition of physiological and other antioxidants to subject's diet.

The argument for the significance to aging of the progressive accumulation of lesions of lipid peroxidation is given much strength by the fact that the above changes are, indeed, characteristic of aging organisms. In particular, intracellular sodium exclusion in cells of aged organisms is reduced (Joseph, 1971). Increased heterogeneity of microsomes and mitochondria has been reported by ourselves (Gordon, 1971) and others (Bertolini, 1969). Microsomes from livers of aged animals have reduced cholesterol content (Hrachovec, 1969). The RNA in microsomes of aged animals is more resistant to exogenous RNAase attack (Gordon, 1971). Microsomes (membrane-bound polysomes) of aged rat brain are different from the young in other, perhaps related, ways. They exhibit an irreversible paradoxical response to rising temperature in vitro in the presence

of cell sap (see Table VI and Note Added in Proof of
Gordon, 1971); they "freeze" or increase in internal hydrogen bond content, as occurs when polymer domains undergo
a net increase in melting of hydration waters relative to
a standard state, which is the standard response to temperature elevation of systems that are increased in hydrophobicity.

Endocrine-effector relations are disturbed in aging
tissues (Gutman, 1970). For example, effector systems for
insulin and catecholamines exhibit a strikingly reduced
sensitivity in whole organs, tissues and homogenates from
aged organisms (Jelinkova et al., 1972; Verzár and Ermini,
1970; Walker and Walker, 1973). The physiological activity
of catecholamines is known to depend upon stereospecific
interactions between hormone and receptor, with the result
that the D-form of optically active catecholamines is many
orders of magnitude less active than the L-form (Gordon
and Zak, 1963). Such signal molecules would be expected
to be vulnerable to the distortion of membrane receptor
areas by local nonfunctional changes in lipid structure,
and consequent alteration in lipid protein interaction
could contribute to the loss in endocrine sensitivity observed.

LIPID PEROXIDATION AND A GENERAL HYPOTHESIS
CONCERNING THE FAILURE OF TRANSMISSION
OF BIOLOGICAL INFORMATION IN AGING

These deteriorative changes generate structures that
are increasingly less able to transmit biological information through the cell substance and across cell interfaces,
and resemble in their consequences events that are held to
be central to aging, according to the "Error Theory of
Aging" advanced by Orgel (1963) and amplified by others
(Burnet, 1973; Holliday and Tarrant, 1972; Wheldon, 1973).
The Orgel and lipid-peroxidation hypotheses can be fruit-
fully compared. According to the Orgel theory, inappropriate nucleotide and amino acid sequences that are generated
as a result of random errors in transcription and translation result, over time, in the accumulation of proteins
that have a reduced functionality. When such proteins
containing inappropriate amino acid sequences include
synthetases and, as faulty enzymes, themselves become involved in the synthesis of other information-bearing

molecules, i.e. messenger RNA or protein, then the rate of accumulation of function-reducing errors in protein synthesis will accelerate, resulting finally in catastrophe.

Because this hypothesis focuses exclusively on amino acid and nucleotide sequences, it describes, in effect, only a special case. A more general source of structural and functional "noise" lies in the disturbance of coacervate, steric, and related cooperative properties in tissue gels, sols, matrices, and surfaces. These properties, which emerge from specific organization, certainly modulate membrane enzyme action, recognition, reception and transport phenomena as significantly as specific nucleotide or amino acid sequences do. When they are disturbed by random destructive cytoplasmic events, such as the peroxidation of lipid components et sequentia, even correctly programmed protein enzymes, endocrine receptors or modulators of facilitated transport that are adjacent, can become nonfunctional. An acceleration is built into this kind of information failure as well, satisfying the Gompertzian character of aging.

ANTIOXIDANT EFFECTS IN AGING

In the mainstream of studies concerning the significance of free radical formation in aging organisms is work examining the effects of vitamin E and chemically unrelated antioxidants on the aging process. Since it is agreed that chemically dissimilar antioxidants, such as the tocopherols, vitamin C, glutathione, selenoamino acids and butylated hydroxytoluene, can suppress the lipid peroxidation of biological membranes in in vitro systems (Green, 1972; Milvy, 1973), the degree to which retardation of aging phenomena in living organisms can be affected by these compounds has been of central interest to workers in this area of gerontology. Results to date can be summed up as follows:

1) Reducing compounds significantly prolong the life spans of flies (Miquel, personal communication).

2) Harman (1968) finds such reducing agents to increase the mean life span of one strain of mouse.

3) In studies by Tappel, et al. (1973), the life span

70

of another strain of mouse was not increased, although significant antioxidant effects were exerted in several tissues.

In the Tappel study, however, the accumulation of peroxidized lipopigment that occurred in testis and heart from age 7 to 22 months was significantly reduced by the addition of a high, but nontoxic, level of antioxidant mixtures to the diet. In this study, mortality and several fitness measures were shown not to be affected by this change in diet. Interestingly, in contrast to other species studied (Nandy, 1968; Reichel et al., 1968; Zeman, 1971), in the mouse strain examined by the Tappel group (Tappel et al., 1973) accumulation of peroxidized age pigment in the central nervous system did not strikingly increase with age and could not be determined to be significantly reduced by the addition of antioxidants to the diet.

The great body of evidence does indicate that the accumulation of peroxidized lipofuscin pigments in the central nervous system is covariant with the aging of this organ in various rodents and dogs. There is other intriguing work which finds that these processes and animal death, as well, can be significantly suppressed by drugs. An evaluation of these data, which concerns lipofuscin, first requires that we briefly review what is known about these pigments.

LIPOFUSCIN: A PRODUCT OF LIPID PEROXIDATION AND FREE RADICAL ATTACK

That lipofuscin pigments accumulate in many organs with the aging of the organism is not disputed. Pigmented material of this nature has been determined by histochemical, analytical chemical, and fluorimetric techniques to be rich in lipids and proteins, to be in an abnormally conjugated and cross-linked state, and to exhibit fluorescence characteristics which, as stated above, can be duplicated by the peroxidation of polyunsaturated lipids (Strehler, 1964; Tappel, 1972, 1973). This age pigment has its richest deposit with aging in rodent testis, in which polyunsaturated fat levels are very high (Tappel, 1973). In guinea pigs and dogs, the accumulation of this pigment is progressive with age in brain, testis and heart, among other tissues; and, in flies, one observes such accumulation during aging in the gastrointestinal tract. The age-dependent accumulation of lipofuscin pigments, which many take to be an accumulation of products peroxidizing poly-unsaturated fatty acids, is not accompanied by a change in the average composition of saturated and unsaturated fats, as reported for liver.

While lipofuscin, then, does not represent an attack on the net polyunsaturated fatty acid compartment, hypotheses have been offered, based on different bodies of data that these pigments take origin from a peroxidation of components of the polyunsaturated fatty acid that are minor in quantity relative to total, but important in that they are located in mitochondrial membranes or, alternatively, on the endoplasmic reticulum of cells (Strehler, 1964).

While it is widely accepted that mammalian lipofuscin pigments originate from subcellular organelles undergoing peroxidation reactions, it has recently been observed that similar pigments are produced in aging fruit flies at a far more rapid rate. Further evidence offered by Miquel, et al. (1974) indicates that, in the pigment of Drosophila melanogaster, lysosomes participate in the evolution of lipofuscin by engulfing the damaged membranes. The debris is held to accumulate within lysosomes because the cross-linked protein fractions cannot be fully hydrolyzed by lysosomal proteolytic enzymes. Interestingly, these products of lipid peroxidation, which accumulate too rapidly in flies, may fill up to 50% of the cytoplasmic volume in certain organs, whereas the maximum amount of lipofuscin in a human tissue may be of the order of 5% (Reichel et al., 1968).

Whether lipofuscin does more than reflect intracellular damage, or whether its presence contributes damage per se, is unresolved (Reichel et al., 1968; Zeman, 1971). The observation has been made that much lipofuscin can accumulate in nerve cells without apparent reduction in their function. At some extreme, lipofuscin accumulation in cells with aging should reduce the density of space-occupying, synthesizing and metabolizing organelles and, as well, generate a series of free-energy barriers that impede the diffusion and transport of essential metabolites and information-bearing molecules across the domains that they occupy.

This may explain the correlation that develops between lipofuscin deposition in neurons and functional

deficit in advanced stages of Batten-Vogt syndrome and
juvenile amaurotic idiocy in English setters (Zeman, 1971),
which are diseases of peroxidized lipofuscin deposition in
humans and canines, respectively.

CENTROPHENOXINE: AN EXPERIMENTAL DRUG AFFECTING LIPOFUSCIN

Although it is widely assumed that lipofuscin is a
form of intracellular debris that cannot be metabolized,
an interesting group of papers suggests that lipofuscin is
not an immodifiable end product. These papers concern the
actions of the drug Centrophenoxine (which is the p-chloro-
phenoxyacetyl ester of dimethylaminoethanol) and dimethylaminoethanol (as the acetamidobenzoate salt).

In further studies developed from earlier work by
Nandy and Bourne (1966), Nandy (1968) reports that Centrophenoxine, injected intramuscularly or intraperitoneally
into guinea pigs aged 6 months to 6 years at a dose of
80 mg/kg for 4-12 weeks, reduces the deposition of lipofuscin that has occurred in guinea pig brain, with effects
being maximal after 12 weeks of treatment; and this is in
association with effects on several brain enzyme systems.
Glycolytic metabolism is shifted away from the Emden-
Myerhoff systems and towards the pentose phosphate-shunt
pathway, which should increase the availability of reducing
cofactors, such as NADH and NADPH, which compounds are
important in phospholipid synthesis. Cytoplasmic simple
esterase and acid phosphatase activities are reduced in
brain; this, according to one view (Hochschild, 1973a, b),
may reflect a reduction in lysosome dissolution.

Hochschild (1973a) has given Centrophenoxine to male
Swiss-Webster mice aged 8.6 months, as a 2.03% solution in
their drinking water over 24 months. Under these conditions, the labile ester bond in Centrophenoxine is hydrolyzed, with the result that a mixture of phenoxyacetic acid
and dimethylaminoethanol is the medication ingested by the
animals. In this experiment, lipofuscin in brain was not
affected by therapy, while the accumulation of lipofuscin
in heart was reduced. Dimethylaminoethanol and p-chloro-
phenoxyacetic acid increased the median, mean and maximum
survival time from the start of drug administration by
29.5%, 27.3% (P = 0.029), and 39.7%, respectively. In a
second study, Hochschild (1973b) gave 20-22-month-old A/J

mice only dimethylaminoethanol, as the acetamidobenzoate salt, and observed a similar prolongation of the remainder of their life span.

These studies indicate that the laying down of lipofuscin pigment during aging can be retarded and even reversed by chemical agents other than antioxidants, and that such effects, when observed only outside the central nervous system, were covariant with prolongation of life in two mouse strains. The difference in drug effect on brain lipofuscin, as found by Nandy and Bourne (1966) and by Hochschild (1973a, b), may be due either to unique central effects of the intact Centrophenoxine ester or to probable higher drug levels in brain following the parenteral injection of drug by Nandy.

The apparent reversal of lipofuscin deposition is fascinating, and indicates that latent lipofuscin scavenging mechanisms may be activated, to the advantage of the aging organism. Whether these important observations will be reproduced and, if so, whether, in mice, the dimethylaminoethanol effect on life span will be found causally relatable to lipofuscin pigment clearance anywhere is, of course, not known at this time.

ISOPRINOSINE: AN EXPERIMENTAL DRUG AFFECTING ORGANELLES

We have previously developed (United States Patent #3,646,007) and reported on (Gordon and Brown, 1972; Gordon and Ronsen, 1970) a compound that has a significant relationship to dimethylaminoethanol and, thus, to Centrophenoxine. This is methisoprinol (Isoprinosine), which is a complex containing 3 moles of dimethylaminoisopropanol (as the acetamidobenzoate salt) to 1 mole of inosine. While we have not studied effects of its chronic administration on lipofuscin pigments, we have shown that Isoprinosine partially reverses the deteriorated brain functioning of aged rats as determined in avoidance learning systems (Gordon, 1971), while increasing the rate of turnover of microsomal and ribosomal RNA and decreasing structural heterogeneity in microsomes and ribosomes (Gordon, 1971; Gordon et al., 1974). Furthermore, we have shown that increasing the amount of alkylamino alcohol in this composition increases the rate of microsomal RNA turnover in a dose-dependent way over a basal contribution to

74

enhanced turnover made by inosine (Gordon, 1971).

While lipofuscin pigments may, in part, represent the
terminal "debris" stage of microsomes that have sustained
multiple lipid peroxidations and are no longer contributing
to metabolism, it should be clear that, at an earlier
stage of disorganization, aging microsomes may continue to
function as loci of diverse metabolic events and contribute
to the dysfunction in aging by exhibiting quantitative or
qualitative defects or errors in metabolism, especially in
protein synthesis.

A large body of data describes changes that occur in
the structure and function of brain microsomes with aging,
-- changes that may be attributed to progressive injury of
the type under discussion. Increased hydrophobicity and
increasing structural heterogeneity have already been referred to (Gordon, 1971). A reduced translational activity
has been found by Hrachovec (1969) and Mainwaring (1969)
in liver.

Ribosomes from aged brain exhibit a reduced translational activity, as well as a reduction in the capacity to
discriminate between endogenous and alien messenger RNA
(Gordon et al., 1974). In this work, functioning ribosomes
from very aged rat brain translated exogenous messenger
RNA (polyuridylic acid) more readily, while translating
native messenger RNA less readily, than ribosomes from the
mature non-senile rat. Further, ribosomes from very aged
rats exhibited more orthochromicity -- i.e., were less
compact -- than ribosomes of the mature rat. Such alterations in organization and reduction in translational
capacity may be associated with reduction in host biochemical information flow in the rat brain. On the other
hand, the reduced translational selectivity, i.e. the
increased capacity to translate exogenous or alien messenger RNA, may reflect, as well, a greater openness to the
translation of messenger RNA of virus origin, and thus
further illuminate a new dimension in aging, a contribution
from virus input, that is only now beginning to receive
attention.

In this regard, we note that Isoprinosine, while
partially reversing the aging changes in brain ribosomes
cited above and increasing brain function for certain
learning tasks (Gordon, 1971), also exerts an antiviral
effect (Chang and Weinstein, 1973; Gordon et al., 1974;
Gordon and Brown, 1972; Muldoon et al., 1972). We refer

the reader, as well, to articles that consider links between aging and virus infection (Adler, these proceedings;
Gajdusek, 1967; Gordon, 1971; Gordon et al., 1974).

While enhancing memory formation, the effects of
Isoprinosine on ribosomal structure and function in aging
rat brain are coupled to another effect on RNA metabolism
as observed in vivo. This is an enhanced turnover of
both microsomal and ribosomal RNAs, as described by
Gordon (1971), and as exemplified in figure 1. In this

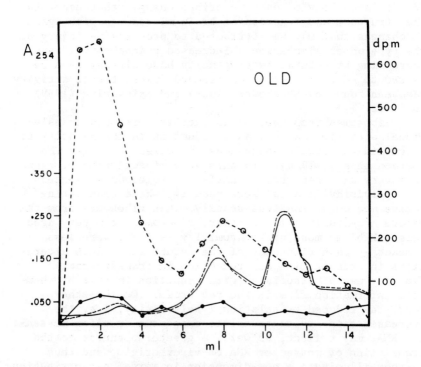

Fig. 1 Animals used were 28-month-old female Sprague-
Dawley rats. Experimental animals ingested approximately
500 mg/kg/24 hours Isoprinosine ad libitum in their drinking water. 24 hours prior to sacrifice, 50 µC H[3]-orotic
acid was injected intracisternally into each rat. In pre-
paring brain polysomes for study, resuspended purified
polysomes (1.0 ml) were incubated with 1.0 ml of 0.1M
Na_2EDTA and 0.25M KCl for 1 hour...(continued on page 77)

Fig. 1 (continued)... at 0-4°C, after which 1.0 ml was
layered on 14 ml linear sucrose density gradients (5-25%
W/V) and centrifuged for 3.5 hours at 27,000 rpm in the
SW-27 rotor of a Beckman L2 centrifuge. The 40S and 60S
subunits were found to locate at 57% (8 ml) and 75% (11 ml)
of the sucrose gradient, respectively. Control optical
density, ——; treated optical density, -----; control
disintegrations per minute, ●; treated disintegrations per
minute, o.

work, the polysomes from the brains of control and drug-
treated 28-month-old female Sprague-Dawley rats were separated into subunits and messenger RNAs by Na_2EDTA pretreat-
ment and sucrose density gradient ultracentrifugation. This
effect indicates that free ribosomes and those of microsomes have a shorter functional life span under the influence of drug treatment.

While Hochschild (1973a, b) proposes that, as a result
of input from alkylamino alcohols, lysosomal membranes may
be stabilized and leak fewer catabolic enzymes to impair
membrane function in aging, we suggest that an equally
significant role may be played by the enhancement of active
repair mechanisms. Specifically, we suggest that input
enhancing the turnover of microsomal and ribosomal RNA in
aging rat brain may be associated with a general acceleration in turnover of these domains and, by this effect, may
facilitate the catabolism and clearance of organelle
domains that have been injured by free radical lipid peroxidation or attack on nucleic acids, but which remain as
loci of dysfunction. Note that, as reported by Comoli and
coworkers (1972), whole membranes and major macromolecular
components turn over synchronously in aging lysosomes and
microsomes.

A POTENTIAL RELATION BETWEEN
BIOCHEMICAL AND BEHAVIORAL STIMULATION

In connection with organelle turnover, I wish to call
attention to the finding of my collaborator, Dr. Barbara
Doty Lowther (1966), that rats age more slowly, i.e. do not
develop memory deficits and gain less added weight, if
they live the second year of their life in a stimulating

environment rather than in a standard rat cage (Table I). Behaviorally, these "enriched" rats resemble rats aged in a standard environment that are subsequently given Isoprinosine.

TABLE I

Delayed Avoidance Performance[a] of Animals Reared in Enriched Environments[b] or Treated with Isoprinosine[c]

| | | Mean Trials to Criterion | |
Cage Type	Treatment	Acquisition	Relearning
Standard	Saline	141.6[d]	86.3[d]
Standard	Isoprinosine 400 mg/kg	110.9	72.4
Standard	Isoprinosine 250 mg/kg	104.7	68.9
Enriched	Saline	98.5	66.2
Enriched	Isoprinosine	91.8[e]	59.7

[a]Criterion for the conditioned avoidance learning task was 5 correct avoidances out of 10 consecutive responses; animals ran 30 trials per day. The task is further described by Doty (1966).

[b]Enrichment involved rearing for the second year in a large group environment, 4 feet in diameter, filled with an assortment of small stimulus objects; for example, children's toys, mirrors, brushes and tin cans. All animals were reared for the first year and standard cage animals were reared for the second year as well, in a 12-inch mesh cage without objects. Same-sexed animals were reared together.

[c]Isoprinosine was given orally late in the learning consolidation period, 2 hours after the end of trials each day.

[d]Significantly larger than all other group means; $P < 0.01$.

[e]Significantly smaller than means of all groups reared in standard cages; $P < 0.01$.

What has happened in the brains of behaviorally enriched rats? It is well established that, in relatively short-term experiments, environmental stimulation relative to sensory deprivation enhances RNA and protein turnover in rodent and monkey brain (Appel et al., 1967; Talwar et al., 1966). We are led to suggest that, in the Lowther study, brain stimulation relative to the basal condition of monotony may have been associated with an enhanced organelle turnover and reduced accumulation of deteriorating intracellular membranes. One may wonder, finally, whether such a contribution is made to organelles and to longevity, by life stimulation in human aging.

REFERENCES

Appel, S. H., Davis, W. and Scott, S. (1967). Science 157, 836.

Barber, A. A. and Bernheim, F. (1967). Adv. Gerontol. Res. 2, 355.

Bertolini, A. M. (1969). "Gerontologic Metabolism." Charles C. Thomas, Springfield, Illinois.

Bieri, J. G. and Anderson, R. A. (1960). Arch. Biochem. Biophys. 90, 105.

Brooks, A. L., Mead, D. K. and Peters, R. F. (1973). J. Gerontol. 28, 452.

Bunyan, J., Cawthorne, M. A., Diplock, A. T. and Green, J. (1969). Brit. J. Nutr. 23, 309.

Burnet, F. M. (1973). Lancet 2, 480.

Chang, T. W. and Weinstein, L. (1973). Am. J. Med. Sci. 265, 143.

Commoner, B., Heise, J. J., Lippincot, B. B., Norberg, R. E., Passoneau, J. V. and Townsend, J. (1957). Science 126, 57.

Comoli, R., Ferioli, M. E. and Azzola, S. (1972). Exp. Gerontol. 7, 369.

Demopoulos, H. B. (1973a). Fed. Proc. 32, 1859.

Demopoulos, H. B. (1973b). Fed. Proc. 32, 1903.

Demopoulos, H. B. (1973c). (Chairman, Symposium on Free Radical Pathology, 54th Annual Meeting, Federation of American Societies for Experimental Biology.) Fed. Proc. 32, 1859.

Di Luzio, N. R. (1973). Fed. Proc. 32, 1875.

Doty, B. (1966). J. Gerontol. 21, 287.

Gajdusek, D. C. (1967). New Engl. J. Med. 276, 392.

Goldstein, B. D., Lodi, C., Collinson, C. and Balchum, O.
  J. (1969). Arch.Environ. Health 18, 631.
Gordon, P. (1971). Adv. Gerontol. Res. 3, 199.
Gordon, P. and Brown, E. R. (1972). Can. J. Microbiol. 18,
  1463.
Gordon, P. and Ronsen, B. (1970). Fed. Proc. 29, 684.
Gordon, P., Ronsen, B. and Brown, E. R. (1974). Antimicro-
  biol. Ag. Chemother. 5, 153.
Gordon, P. and Zak, R. (1963). Science 140, 294.
Green, J. (1972). Ann. N. Y. Acad. Sci. 203, 29.
Gutman, E. (1970). Exp. Gerontol. 5, 357.
Harman, D. (1956). J. Gerontol. 11, 298.
Harman, D. (1961). J. Gerontol. 16, 247.
Harman, D. (1962). Radiation Res. 16, 753.
Harman, D. (1968). J. Gerontol. 23, 476.
Harman, D. and Piette, L. H. (1966). J. Gerontol. 21, 560.
Hochschild, R. (1973a). Exp. Gerontol. 8, 117.
Hochschild, R. (1973b). Exp. Gerontol. 8, 185.
Holliday, R. and Tarrant, G. M. (1972). Nature 238, 26.
Hrachovec, J. P. (1969). Gerontologia 15, 52.
Ingram, D. J. E. (1958). "Free Radicals as Studied by
  Electron Spin Resonance." Academic Press, New York.
Jelinkova, M., Stuchlikova, E., Hruza, Z., Deyl, Z. and
  Smrz, M. (1972). Exp. Gerontol. 7, 263.
Joseph. N. R. (1971). "Physical Chemistry of Aging," Vol.8
  in Interdisciplinary Topics in Gerontology (H. T.
  Blumenthal, ed.), S. Karger, Basel, Switzerland.
Lucy, J. A. (1972). Ann. N. Y. Acad. Sci. 203, 4.
Mainwaring, W. I. P. (1969). Biochem. J. 113, 869.
Medvedev, Z. A. (1964). Adv. Gerontol. Res. 1, 181.
Milvy, P. (1973). Fed. Proc. 32, 1895.
Miquel, J. (1973). Personal communication.
Miquel, J., Tappel, A. L., Dillard, C. J., Herman, M. M.
  and Bensch, K. G. (1974). Submitted for publication.
Muldoon, R. L., Mezny, L. and Jackson, G. G. (1972). Anti-
  microbiol. Ag. Chemother. 2, 224.
Myers, L. S., Jr. (1973). Fed. Proc. 32, 1882.
Nair. P. O. and Kayden, H. J. (eds.) (1972). "Vitamin E
  and Its Role in Cellular Metabolism." New York Academy
  of Sciences International Conference. Ann. N. Y. Acad.
  Sci. 203, 1.
Nandy, K. (1968). J. Gerontol. 23, 82.
Nandy, K. and Bourne, G. H. (1966). Nature 210, 313.
Orgel, L. E. (1963). Proc. Natl. Acad. Sci. 49, 517.

Packer, L., Deamer, D. W. and Heath, R. L. (1967). _Adv. Gerontol. Res._ 2, 108.

Pryor, W. A. (1973). _Fed. Proc._ 32, 1862.

Reichel, W., Hollander, J., Clark, J. H. and Strehler, B. L. (1968). _J. Gerontol._ 23, 71.

Seligman, M. L. and Demopoulos, H. B. (1973). _Ann. N. Y. Acad. Sci._ 222, 640.

Strehler, B. L. (1964). _Adv. Gerontol. Res._ 1, 343.

Talwar, G. P., Goel, B. K., Chopra, S. P. and D'Monte, B. (1966). _In_ "Macromolecules and Behavior" (J. Gaito, ed.) pp. 71-88, Meredith Publishing Co. (Appleton-Century-Crofts), New York.

Tappel, A. L. (1965). _Fed. Proc._ 24, 73.

Tappel, A. L. (1972). _Ann. N. Y. Acad. Sci._ 203, 12.

Tappel, A. L. (1973). _Fed. Proc._ 32, 1870.

Tappel, A. L., Fletcher, B. and Deamer, D. (1973). _J. Gerontol._ 28, 415.

Verzár, F. and Ermini, M. (1970). _Gerontologia_ 16, 223.

Walker, J. B. and Walker, J. P. (1973). _Brain Res._ 54, 391.

Wallace, J. D., Driscoll, D. H., Kalomiris, C. G. and Neaves, A. (1970). _Cancer_ 25, 1087.

Wheldon, T. E. (1973). _Lancet_ 2, 616.

Wills, E. D. (1970). _Intern. J. Radiation Biol._ 17, 217.

Zeman, W. (1971). _Adv. Gerontol. Res._ 3, 147.

CYTOGERONTOLOGY

Leonard Hayflick, Ph.D.

Department of Medical Microbiology
Stanford University School of Medicine
Stanford, California 94305

INTRODUCTION

The processes of aging are responsible for the only
fatal disease to which all of us are destined to succumb.
Yet the fundamental causes of biological aging are almost
as much a mystery today as they have ever been. Within
the past decade, however, gerontologists have made a
number of observations that lead to some intriguing in-
sights into the biological mechanisms that underly the
phenomenon of animal senescence generally and human senescence in particular.

How remarkable it is that despite the universality of
the problem, it has occupied and still does the attention
of very few biologists. It is a certainty that the amount
of research done on the basic mechanisms of biological
aging is inversely proportional to its importance. Consider
the fact that even if the current national effort to
understand and to cure all human cancers was to be successful, life expectancy at birth would be increased by only
about two years (Siegel and O'Leary, 1973). In addition
to this, if cardiovascular diseases--the leading killer--
were to be miraculously eliminated, then about seventeen
more years of life could be expected. Such a fortunate
generation of Americans in which the two major causes of
death were eliminated would, surprisingly, enjoy only
nineteen years of additional life expectancy (Table I).
Yet the human life span itself would be unaffected. More
people would simply be reaching the maximum limit. We are
led, inescapably, to conclude that research on specific
diseases that might lead to their control would not
lengthen the human life span. Indeed, regardless of the

state of technological or medical progress within a country, the human life span of ninety years or so is similar in all societies and has, apparently, never changed throughout recorded history. What has changed is the probability of dying in younger age groups.

TABLE I

Gain in Expectation of Life at Birth and at Age 65 due to Elimination of Various Causes of Death

Cause of Death	Gain in years in expectation of life if cause was eliminated	
	At Birth	At Age 65
Major cardiovascular-renal diseases	10.9	10.0
Heart disease	5.9	4.9
Vascular diseases affecting the central nervous system	1.3	1.2
Malignant neoplasms	2.3	1.2
Accidents excluding those caused by motor vehicles	0.6	0.1
Motor vehicle accidents	0.6	0.1
Influenza & pneumonia	0.5	0.2
Infectious diseases (excluding tuberculosis)	0.2	0.1
Diabetes mellitus	0.2	0.2
Tuberculosis	0.1	0.0

Source: Life tables published by the National Center of Health Statistics, USPHS and U. S. Bureau of the Census, "Some Demographic Aspects of Aging in the United States," February 1973.

The more advantaged societies are therefore composed of a greater number of individuals who are likely to reach the maximum life span. This is illustrated in figure 1. A further extension of this dialectic would mean that if all of the diseases to which man is prone are resolved the ultimate rectangular survival curve (figure 1) would be achieved with a maintenance of youthful vigor, and freedom from both organic and infectious diseases resulting in sudden death occurring at the stroke of midnight on, say, our one hundredth birthday. This observation is not made lightly for it is clear that this is the direction in which we are moving unless the non-disease producing fundamental biological causes of aging are better understood.

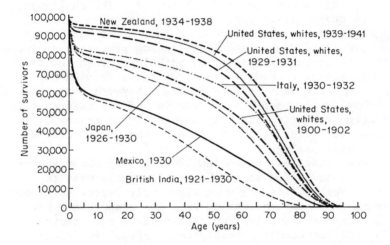

Fig. 1 Number of survivors of 100,000 male live births from life-tables for selected countries. From: "Ageing: The Biology of Senescence", by Alex Comfort. Copyright 1965, 1964 by Alex Comfort. Reprinted by permission of Holt, Rinehart & Winston, Inc.

If it is our intention to extend what now appears to be a fixed life span for the human species, then the trivial amount of support and effort now directed toward an understanding of the biological mechanisms underlying age changes seems to me to be wholly incapable of reaching such a lofty goal.

To presume that the resolution of all disease states would result in sudden death on our one hundredth birthday also implies that the fundamental causes of aging are expressed suddenly, are essentially noncumulative over a long span of time, and are irreversible. In comparison with most other normal biological processes, there is real doubt that normal aging occurs so suddenly. For example, late occurring non-disease-related normal biological processes, such as the menopause and the graying of the hair, are not sudden events.

One must therefore conclude that if all disease-related causes of death were to be resolved, then the aging processes would present some clear physical manifestations well in advance of death itself. The challenge, then, is obviously to separate disease-related changes from the basic biological changes that are a part of the aging process. Since fundamental aging processes do indeed contribute to the expression of pathology, then the two concepts may be so closely intertwined as to make any clear, semantic distinctions futile. Nevertheless, the two examples of menopause and graying of the hair that I have cited are not ordinarily thought of as states of disease but rather as early signs of the normal processes of biological aging.

These examples are chosen because they occur subsequent to that period in the human life cycle when reproductive capabilities are most vigorously expressed. Indeed, it seems quite apparent that, from the standpoints both of evolution and survival of the species, age-related biological decrements probably occur after reproductive maturation. Personally, I do not agree at all with the frequently stated notion that aging begins at conception. In the sense that the genetic program for age changes may be set at that time, there is no contest; however, it would be more accurate to say that biological manifestations of age changes generally occur subsequent to the time that species members reach reproductive maturity.

Although life expectancy at birth has increased in recent years at age sixty-five to seventy, it has remained essentially fixed. From data similar to those expressed in figure 1 and Table II, we have learned that as various diseases come under control, the survival curves become more rectangular, but all terminate at the same point. The human life span therefore will not be significantly

TABLE II

The Finite Lifetime of Cultured Normal Embryonic
Human and Animal Fibroblasts

Species	Range of population doublings for cultured normal embryo fibroblasts	Maximum Life span in years	Reference
Galapagos Tortoise	90-125	175(?)	Goldstein, 1974
Man	40-60	110	Hayflick and Moorhead, 1961
Chicken	15-35	30	Hay and Strehler, 1967 Pontén, 1970 Lima and Macieira-Coelho, 1974 Harris, 1957
Mouse	14-28	3.5	Todaro and Green, 1963 Rothfels et al., 1963

87

changed until the underlying, non-disease related, biological causes of senescence are either slowed or stopped.
Recent assessment of the claims for extreme longevity of
the Abkhasians (residents of the Caucasus) and others
reputed to live from 120 to 160 years are unacceptable to
critical gerontologists (Leaf, 1973a, 1973b, 1973c). Reports of extreme longevity make for good newspaper copy
throughout the world, especially in the Soviet Union where
human interest stories are rarely reported. The ages of
these people have been taken as an article of faith by ob-
servers who fail to adhere to critical standards of scientific evidence. Wholly authentic data on the life span of
man do not reveal life spans beyond 110 to 120 years
(Comfort, 1964) and studies of the Abkhasians, using rigid
rules of evidence, have largely exploded the myth of their
reputed longevity (McKain, 1967; Sachuk, 1964; Chebotarev
and Sachuk, 1964; Hayflick, 1974). Overstatement of ages
seems to be particularly popular among those over 100,
apparently because of the prestige and public attention
that the exaggeration attracts (McKain, 1967). It is all
the easier to do because very few people are around to
challenge the claim. It is perhaps of interest to note
the inconsistency that although life expectancy at birth is
greater in the United States than in the U.S.S.R., it is
greater at ages 60 to 80 in the U.S.S.R. than in the United
States (McKain, 1967).

HYPOTHESES

There is probably no other area of scientific inquiry
that abounds with as many untested or untestable theories
as does the biology of aging. Three of the most tenable
hypotheses on which most other theories ultimately rest are
based on those modern triumphs of intellect that have resulted in our understanding of the molecular biology of the
genetic apparatus. Several considerations, not the least
of which is the constancy of the life span within each
animal species, lead to the conclusion that the probable
cause of senescent change is somehow contained in the
genetic message. Three generalized possibilities are now
au courant. First, that the manifestations of senescent
changes are the result of the playing out of the genetic
program which contains specific information or "aging
genes" that code for the senile changes presaging death of

88

the organism. All developmental changes that take place
can be considered to result from a pre-existing genetic
program that plays out as a function of time. Consider,
for example, the inevitability and predictability of the
occurrence of the menopause, one of several examples which
could be given of a biological event whose expression
occurs late in life, is predictable and is probably genetically based. It is conjectured by the advocates of the
theory of a pre-written genetic program that manifestations
of aging are the result of this kind of mechanism. They
argue further that the survival of a species depends on
the ability of its members to survive long enough to reach
the age of procreation and that what occurs after that is
essentially irrelevant. The biological changes that occur
during this irrelevant period we recognize as senescence.
Indeed, this reasoning has been further extended to argue
that profound clinical manifestations of aging occur only
in man and in his domestic or zoo animals. Animals, it is
maintained, that remain free in nature and have not, like
man, learned to cope with disease and predators do not
exhibit senescent changes to the degree observed in man or
those species he chooses to protect. In the wild, aging
older animals are simply culled by predators and disease
well before significant age-associated biological decrements become manifest. Thus it would be argued, the profound senile changes seen in man are actually artifacts of
civilization and inadvertently unmasked because of man's
success in controlling his environment. A second hypothesis involving the genetic apparatus has many of the
features of the preceding argument, except that specific
"aging genes" do not exist; the organism simply runs out of
genetic information, the result of which are those biological changes that we recognize as senescence.

The third hypothesis of aging now embraced by a large
community of gerontologists maintains that the genetic
apparatus, although admittedly programming for sequential
biological events, does not include a program for senescent
changes per se, but that self-duplicating molecules simply
accumulate inaccurate information or mis-specified proteins. The loss of accurate or reliable information is
seen to occur from an accumulation of random events which
damage the essential information-containing molecules.
When a threshold of "hits", "damage", "insults", or
"errors" is reached, normal biological activities cease

and the manifestation of age-related changes then become evident. The precise nature of damage to such essential molecules is not clearly understood, but the fact of their occurrence is known. Furthermore, systems for repairing some of these mis-specified macromolecules are known and one might account for the broad range of life spans in animal species as equivalent to the degree of perfection evolved by their repair systems. Medvedev has conjectured that the reason for the known great duplication of identical message units in human DNA, for example, is simply the result of the vulnerability to errors inherent in this system, and that the presence of highly redundant information would serve to lengthen the time necessary for "hits", "errors", etc., to accumulate and completely confound the message bit (Medvedev, 1972).

A specialized case of this general theory is that of Orgel, who envisions an ultimate error accumulation in those molecules that produce enzymes (Orgel, 1963). A faulty enzyme could very quickly result in a catastrophic burst of nonsense or even lethal mis-specified proteins, very much as a single faulty machine tool would produce hundreds of successive faulty parts. Errors in protein synthesis, including enzymes, may not necessarily be the result of defects in DNA. Instead, age-dependent errors may occur, for example, in the synthetase enzymes involved in the assembly of amino acid chains into proteins on the RNA template. A defect in a synthetase could cause an enzyme to lose its specificity for a given amino acid. This could result in an "error catastrophe" resulting in synthesis of mis-specified proteins. A search for these mis-specified proteins in aging cells is now the subject of considerable research effort. Since no system works flawlessly, what causes these defects to occur initially? Is it by chance or programming by "aging genes" which, like a clock mechanism, assures that the genetic program functions accurately to a point and then specifies its ending?

Whether any of the aforementioned notions alone, in combination or not at all will ultimately explain the biology of senescence cannot now be determined. Nevertheless, most gerontologists would argue that the fundamental events which orchestrate age-related changes are likely to be found in the genetic machinery.

CURRENT RESEARCH IN AGING

Biological research in senescence can be divided into
two broad categories, descriptive and hypothesis testing.
Most investigators believe that the era of descriptive
research in gerontology is ending. A voluminous literature
now exists describing age-related changes at the cell,
tissue, organ and whole animal level for many species
including man. The likelihood that these descriptive
studies, if continued, will yield any meaningful clues as
to mechanism is unlikely. Rather, attention now is being
focused on the formulation and testing of hypotheses.
Other than those hypotheses rooted in genetic mechanisms
and described above, several theories of aging currently
under study involve events occurring at a higher organiza-
tional level than the gene or enzyme. These theories
include immunological mechanisms (Walford, 1969), a mechanism based on the age-accelerating effect of radiation
energy (Curtis, 1966), the effect of free-radicals (Harman,
1968) and changes in collagen chemistry (Kohn, 1971). Yet
all of these considerations involve events occurring at
levels of biological complexity that either do not apply
to all animals which age or are secondary or tertiary
changes manifest by fundamental events occurring at the
gene level.

AGING OF CULTURED HUMAN CELLS

Of those observations made in the past ten years that
bear on our understanding of the biology of aging, technological developments allowing for the growth of cultured
cells appear to have contributed significant new knowledge.
Just as cell culture revolutionized virology in the 1950's
and cytogenetics in the 1960's, many believe that gerontology will be the benefactor in the 1970's. The early
developments in this field occurred more than fifty years
ago when an inverse relationship was found between the
"growth rate" of embryonic chicken fibroblasts cultured in
plasma clots and the age of the chicken supplying the
plasma (Carrel and Ebeling, 1921). A few years later, it
was found that the latent period preceding the first
appearance of cells migrating from tissue scraps grown
in vitro increased as a function of donor age (Suzuki,
1925; Goldschmidt et al., 1937). The last observation

made prior to the renaissance of cell culture techniques which occurred in 1950, was the finding of Carrel purportedly showing that fibroblasts grown from a chicken's heart could proliferate indefinitely in culture (Ebeling, 1913; Parker, 1961). Since 1950, the first two observations have been confirmed but the last, and by far the most important to gerontologists, has not. In fact, quite the opposite is now known to be true.

The notion that isolated animal cells in culture are capable of unlimited proliferation profoundly influenced thinking on many fundamental biological questions, not the least of which were theories of senescence. Indeed, it was once thought that animal cells placed in culture will go on to multiply indefinitely if proper cultural conditions were provided. It is now known that this is not the case. It is a rare event when human or animal cells are found to acquire spontaneously the property of unlimited capability for division in vitro. Furthermore, such cells are inevitably abnormal in one or more properties and often resemble cancer cells. Since aging is a property of normal cells in vivo, it follows that we should be studying similar cells in vitro. The importance of a correct understanding of this point cannot be over-emphasized because the apparent indefinite multiplication of isolated vertebrate cells in culture has often been cited as evidence for the thesis that aging in higher animals results from interactions at the supracellular level. In fact, immortality in vitro is a property of abnormal, not normal, cells.

Ten years ago we showed that normal human cells do have a limited ability to proliferate in vitro and interpreted this to be an expression of human aging at the level of a single cell (Hayflick and Moorhead, 1961). We further suggested that manifestations of aging might very well have an intracellular basis and, in particular, might involve the cell genome (Hayflick and Moorhead, 1961; Hayflick, 1965).

Consequently, arguments marshalled against cellular theories of aging that are based on the myth of "immortal" cell cultures must be re-evaluated since those cells that proliferate indefinitely in vitro are abnormal and often behave like cancer cells. Contrariwise, normal cells in vitro do have a finite life span as do the animals from which such cells have been taken. There is no confirmed evidence that normal cells can be maintained in a state of active proliferation in cell culture for a period of time in excess of the specific age of the species from which the cells were obtained. It is also the case that non-dividing highly differentiated normal cells also cannot be maintained in their functional state _in vitro_ in excess of the mean life span of the species from which they were obtained. This is important because functional decrements in non-dividing cells are clearly manifestations of age changes.

It is our contention that _in vitro_ vertebrate senescence phenomena at the level of the cell also occur _in vitro_ when the proper systems are compared. In earlier work with normal human embryonic diploid cell strains, derived from lung tissue, we observed that after a period of active multiplication, generally less than one year, these cells demonstrated an increased doubling time (normally 24 hours), gradual cessation of mitotic activity, accumulation of cellular debris and ultimately total degeneration of the culture (Hayflick and Moorhead, 1961). This phenomenon, called Phase III, is now a common observation by cell culturists when growing normal cells from many types of human and animal tissues. When derived from normal human foetal tissue, the cultured fibroblast populations undergo about fifty population doublings over a period of about six months. We view this finitude as an innate characteristic of all normal cells grown _in vitro_. In order to distinguish that area of gerontological research associated with studies of cultured cells, I would like to suggest the name "cytogerontology". This would separate such studies from those done at levels of greater complexity _in vivo_ and at the supracellular level.

SENESCENCE OF NORMAL CELLS DERIVED FROM DIFFERENT ANIMAL SPECIES

A phenomenon that is fundamental to our understanding of this biology of aging is that interspecies differences in life spans are far greater than individual intraspecies differences. A fruit fly is ancient in 40 days, a mouse at 3 years, a horse at 30, a man at 100 and some tortoise species not until about 150 years (Comfort, 1964). Although for man we are preoccupied with the variability within a species and would like to know how far it can be stretched, I believe that our understanding would be furthered best by inquiring into the mechanism that sets the life span of

each species in a relatively narrow range and on a scale
that embraces several centuries. Only recently have sufficient in vitro studies been done with the cells of several
different animal species to provide us with a clue to this
intriguing question. Table II summarizes this data.

In my view, the likelihood that animals age because
one or more important cell populations lose their proliferative capacity is very unlikely. I would rather suggest
that, as we have shown, normal cells have a finite capacity
for replication, and that this finite limit is rarely, if
ever, reached by cells in vivo but is, of course, demon-
strable in vitro. I would further suggest that functional
losses that occur in cells prior to their loss of division
capacity produce age changes in animals much before their
normal cells have reached their maximum division limit.
Indeed, we are now becoming more aware of many functional
changes taking place in normal human cells grown in vitro
and expressed well before they lose their capacity to
replicate (Holeckova and Cristofalo, 1970; Houck et al.,
1971; Cristofalo et al., 1970). It is more reasonable to
suggest that those subtler changes which herald the
approach of loss of division capacity play a greater role
in the expression of aging and result in death of the
individual animal well before his cells fail to divide. As
we have pointed out before (Hayflick, 1970), the in vitro
endpoint measured by us as loss of capacity for division
is simply a very convenient and reproducible system but
may have little to do with the actual cause of in vivo
aging.

However, the measurement of loss of potential for cell
division is, after all, one of many cell functions that
could be studied. If the manifestations of age changes
are due to loss of cell function, other than loss of cell
division, as I believe is more likely, then in vitro
systems are all the more important as model systems. We
must not lose sight of the fact that cell division itself
is one of a number of functional losses occurring as
normal cells proliferate in vitro. In recent years a
lengthening list of functional losses is being attributed
to human diploid cell strains as they age in vitro and it
is more likely that these functional decrements which are
manifest well before loss of capacity for division, result
in the most important age changes in vivo (Cristofalo,
1972). Hopefully these functional decrements will provide

a better basis on which to explain _in vivo_ aging as they become better analyzed and more carefully studied.

CAN CELL DEATH BE NORMAL?

The death of cells and the destruction of tissues and organs is, after all, a normal part of morphogenic or developmental sequences in animals. It is the common method of eliminating organs and tissues that are useful only in the larval or embryonic stages of many animals; for example, the pronephros and mesonephros of higher vertebrates, the tail and gills of tadpoles, larval insect organs and, in many cases, the thymus. The degeneration of cells is an important part of development and it is a widespread occurrence in mammalian cells (Saunders, 1966). During the development of vertebrate limbs, cell death and cell resorption model not only digits but also thigh and upper arm contours (Whitten, 1969). In the limbs of vertebrates the death clocks function on schedule even when heterochronic tissue grafts are made (Saunders and Fallon, 1966). Thus cell death is an intrinsic part of development. To the casual observer the contemplation that normal human embryo cells grown _in vitro_ will die after dividing vigorously for fifty population doublings is difficult to accept. Yet, the same logic that makes acceptable aging and death in whole animals as being universal and inevitable, often results in disbelief when the same phenomenon is seen to occur in cultured cells derived from these animals.

THOUGHTS ON MECHANISM

By what mechanism(s) do normal cells grown _in vitro_ ultimately lose their capacity to divide? If this phenomenon is the _in vitro_ expression of aging at the cellular level and if it corresponds directly to senescence in the whole animal then the genetic theories of aging described earlier may very well apply. Normal cells may cease dividing or functioning _in vitro_ as a result of the ultimate loss of genetic information either as a consequence of the "playing out" of the genetic program, the expression of "genes for aging", or the accumulation of errors or misinformation in information-containing molecules. Biological aging is undoubtedly a vastly complex process when

viewed from the standpoint of the plethora of biological
changes that accompany it. We are put off by its complexity when viewing the phenomenon as we see it in its multi-
ferous manifestations; yet the underlying cause could be
simple and which could, in chain reaction fashion, involve
increasingly higher orders of cell, tissue and organ complexities.

TEST OF THE ERROR HYPOTHESIS

Of the several theories offered to explain biological
aging and the Phase III phenomenon, the recent notion of
Orgel has elicited significant interest (Orgel, 1963, 1970,
1973). This hypothesis suggests that initial translational
mistakes lead to an ever-increasing accumulation of errors
in proteins, ultimately resulting in functional and structural decrements leading to manifestations of aging and
subsequent cell death.

One of several experimental approaches leading to a
direct test of this hypothesis is to utilize viral probes
as a means of determining whether errors in protein synthesis occur at greater rates in older cells. Since viral
replication depends upon the utilization of a significant
proportion of host cell synthetic machinery, it is hypoth-
esized that any potential for error production in an old
cell would be amplified and more easily detected in viral
progeny that replicate in such cells. If accumulation of
errors in the form of abnormal proteins eventually does
cause or contribute to senescence of human and animal
diploid cell strains in vitro, this should be reflected
or amplified in numbers of anomalies of virus replication
and maturation in host cells approaching, or in, Phase III.
This reasoning is the basis on which the following experiments were designed to test the error catastrophe hypothesis of Orgel.

In collaboration with my colleagues, Mr. G. Tomkins
and Dr. E. Stanbridge (Tomkins et al., 1974) we have used
an RNA virus, poliovirus type 1 and a DNA virus, herpesvirus type 1, to test the fidelity of viral protein synthesis, defective assembly of constituent viral components,
and possible alterations in patterns of cytopathology as a
function of in vitro age of normal human diploid cells.
Four virus properties were assessed: (1) amount of virus
produced, (2) pattern of cytopathology, (3) plaque

96

morphology, and (4) analysis of herpesvirus proteins by polyacrylamide gel electrophoresis. The normal human fetal diploid cell strain WI-38 was used.

Infected cultures showed similar cytopathic effects for both viruses replicating in Phase II and Phase III cells. The first appearance of a cytopathic effect and the rate of progression was comparable in all experiments when 0.1 PFU of virus per cell was used as the inoculum. We also assessed the average number of infectious virus particles produced per cell for both poliovirus type 1 and herpesvirus type 1 (Table III). The Phase III cell populations were found to support the production of a similar number of infectious virions per cell as do Phase II cell populations.

TABLE III

Number of Infectious Virions of Poliovirus and Herpesvirus Produced as a Function of Age of WI-38

WI-38 Population Doubling Level[a]	Virus	Average Number of Cells (x 10^6)	Titer $TCID_{50}/ml$[b]	Average Number of Infectious Virions Produced per Cell
18	Polio I	17	$10^{6.9}$	24
20	Polio I	17	$10^{6.7}$	15
53	Polio I	7	$10^{6.3}$	14
54	Polio I	7	$10^{6.3}$	14
20	Herpes I	17	$10^{7.7}$	150
22	Herpes I	15	$10^{7.6}$	130
58	Herpes I	8	$10^{7.8}$	380
60	Herpes I	6	$10^{7.5}$	250

[a]Replicate cultures of senescent cells failed to sub-culture past population doubling 54 for poliovirus and population doubling 60 for herpesvirus. The senescent cells used were from two separate reconstituted frozen ampules.

[b]Mean of three titrations with 6 replicates per titration.

Herpesvirus type 1 produced plaques in WI-38 cells with shapes following the polar direction of the fibro-blasts, and hence were not circular. More than five hundred plaques were examined in Phase II cells, and four hundred in Phase III cells. The virus plaque morphology was homogeneous in all experiments.

Table IV compares the ratio of large and small plaque types for poliovirus 1. Both plaque purified and non-purified virus was used, and as these produced identical plaque size ratios, the combined results are presented. The arbitrarily determined plaque size ratios found were similar for Phase II and Phase III cells.

TABLE IV

Analysis of Poliovirus Plaque Sizes Produced
in Young and Old WI-38

Population Doubling Level[a]	Number of Plaques Examined	Size	Number	Ratio of Large to Small Plaques
20	1306	≥ 3 mm	899	2.3:1
		< 3 mm	407	
54[b]	789	≥ 3 mm	550	2.3:1
		< 3 mm	239	

[a]Virus passed three times in WI-38 at this population doubling level before assay in WI-38 at population doubling level 18-22.

[b]Phase III cells (replicate control cultures failed to reach confluency upon subculture).

A typical result of an analysis of herpesvirus type 1 proteins by polyacrylamide gel electrophoresis is illustrated in figure 2 and shows that identical absorbance profiles are obtained from herpesvirus type 1 produced in Phase II and Phase III cells.

As indicated, the number of infectious virions produced per cell was similar, despite replication in Phase II or Phase III WI-38. Thus, even though Phase III WI-38 cells could no longer replicate, and on attempted subcultures were unable to attach to the glass substrate, they were still able to support the assembly and production of mature infectious virions to the same degree as actively dividing cells in Phase II.

As each culture was infected with approximately 0.1 PFU per cell, the rate of appearance, type, and progression of the cytopathic effect could be compared. No differences were observed at any point for either virus,

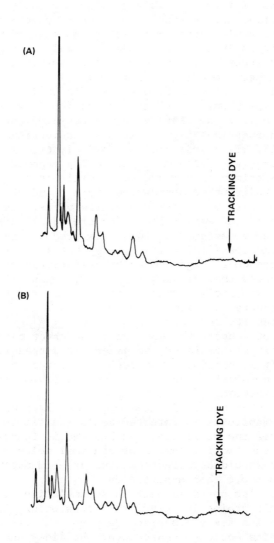

Fig. 2 Absorbance profiles of Coomassie Brilliant Blue-stained herpesvirus type 1 proteins. The virions were produced in Phase II (A) and Phase III (B) cells.

which would suggest that no delay in virus assembly occurred in Phase III cells. This finding was further supported in comparative plaque experiments, where plaque morphology and size were also similar following passage of the virus three times in Phase II and Phase III cells, from a common virus seed stock. No morphological plaque variants were seen in either Phase II or Phase III cells with herpesvirus type 1 and the ratio of plaque sizes in poliovirus infected cells remained constant after replication in Phase II and Phase III cells. No difference was detected when the proteins of herpesvirus type 1 virions replicating in Phase II or Phase III WI-38 were analyzed by polyacrylamide gel electrophoresis. Holland et al.(1973) reported results of similar experiments that are essentially in agreement with ours. In addition to herpesvirus type 1 and poliovirus type 1 they used vesicular stomatitis virus. They showed that Phase II and Phase III cells were equally susceptible to all three viruses, that the virus produced in such cells had the same specific activity, and that senescent cells did not produce a large number of defective virions. They further showed that viruses produced in Phase II and Phase III cells have similar thermal stabilities and that mutation rates were also similar.

Our results and those of Holland et al.(1973), therefore, do not support the concept of an error catastrophe occurring in old cells due to generalized translational errors. It is possible, however, that errors may be restricted to specific host cell codons which do not affect virus replication.

As pointed out by Holland et al. (1973), poliovirus induces a replicase in infected cells (Baltimore et al., 1963) and if the replicases synthesized in Phase III cells contain a substantial number of abnormal molecules, mutation rates should be affected. Our experimental evidence does not support this expectation.

It is also possible that an accumulation of error-containing proteins in aging cells does occur, but since viral proteins are synthesized de novo, the presence of such proteins would go undetected. Holliday and Tarrant (1972) and Lewis and Tarrant (1972) have discussed this possibility when they described a lower specific activity and a higher temperature lability of enzymes found in Phase III human diploid cells as compared with those in Phase II. Although the experiments described here by no means disprove the error hypothesis, our results and those of Holland et al. (1973) do not support it. As discussed previously (Hayflick, 1970, 1972, 1974), we favor an explanation for the Phase III phenomenon, and for biological aging generally, based upon a specific genetic program where, as in normal biological development, gene expression and gene regulation govern the sequential production of information containing molecules. The expression of biological aging may depend upon these same fundamental mechanisms and not upon protein infidelity as the essential cause.

ACKNOWLEDGEMENT

Research reported on in this presentation was supported, in part, by grant HD 04004 from the National Institute of Child Health and Human Development, National Institutes of Health, Bethesda, Maryland.

REFERENCES

Baltimore, D., Eggers, H. J., Franklin, R. M. and Tamm, I. (1963). Proc. Nat. Acad. Sci. (USA) 49, 843.

Carrel, A. and Ebeling, A. H. (1921). J. Exp. Med. 34, 599.

Chebotarev, D. F. and Sachuk, N. N. (1964). J. Gerontol. 19, 435.

Comfort, A. (1964). "Ageing: The Biology of Senescence." Holt, Rinehart and Winston, Inc., New York.

Cristofalo, V. J. (1972). In "Advances in Gerontological Research" (B. L. Strehler, ed.), Vol. 3, Academic Press, New York.

Cristofalo, V. J., Howard, B. V. and Kritchevsky, D. (1970). In "Organic, Biological and Medicinal Chemistry" (V. Gallo and L. Santomarra, eds.), Vol. 2, North Holland Publishers, Amsterdam.

Curtis, H. J. (1966). "Biological Mechanisms of Aging." Chas. C. Thomas, Springfield, Illinois.

Ebeling, A. H. (1913). J. Exp. Med. 17, 273.

Goldschmidt, J., Hoffman, R. and Doljanski, L. (1937). Compt. Rend. Soc. Biol. (Paris) 126, 389.

Goldstein, S. (1974). Exp. Cell Res. (in press).

Harman, D. (1968). J. Gerontol. 23, 476.

Harris, M. (1957). Growth 21, 149.

Hay, R. J. and Strehler, B. L. (1967). Exp. Gerontol. 2, 123.

Hayflick, L. (1965). Exp. Cell Res. 37, 614.
Hayflick, L. (1970). Exp. Gerontol. 5, 291.
Hayflick, L. (1972). In "Aging and Development" (H. Bredt and J. W. Rohen, eds.), Band 4, F. K. Schattauer Verlag, Mainz Academy of Science and Literature, Stuttgart, Germany.
Hayflick, L. (1974). The Gerontologist 14, 37.
Hayflick, L. and Moorhead, P. S. (1961). Exp. Cell Res. 25, 585.
Holeckova, E. and Cristofalo, V. J. (eds.) (1970). "Aging in Cell and Tissue Culture." Plenum Press, New York.
Holland, J. H., Kohne, D. and Doyle, M. V. (1973). Nature (London) 245, 316.
Holliday, R. and Tarrant, G. M. (1972). Nature (London) 238, 26.
Houck, J. C., Sharma, V. K. and Hayflick, L. (1971). Proc. Soc. Exp. Biol. Med. 137, 331.
Kohn, R. R. (1971). "Principles of Mammalian Aging." Prentice Hall, Inc., Englewood Cliffs, N. J.
Leaf, A. (1973a). National Geographic 143. 93.
Leaf. A. (1973b). Sci. Am. 229, 45.
Leaf, A. (1973c). Hospital Practice 8, 75.
Lewis, C. M. and Tarrant, G. M. (1972). Nature (London) 239, 316.
Lima, L. and Macieira-Coelho, A. (1974). Exp. Cell Res. (in press).
McKain, W. C. (1967). The Gerontologist 1, 70.
Medvedev, Z. A. (1972). Exp. Gerontol. 1, 227.
Orgel, L. E. (1963). Proc. Nat. Acad. Sci. (USA) 49, 517.
Orgel, L. E. (1970). Proc. Nat. Acad. Sci. (USA) 67, 1476.
Orgel, L. E. (1973). Nature 243, 441.
Parker, R. C. (1961). "Methods of Tissue Culture." Harper and Row, New York.
Pontén, J. (1970). Intern. J. Cancer 6, 323.
Rothfels, K. H., Kupelwieser, E. B. and Parker, R. C. (1963). Can. Cancer Conf. 5, 191.
Sachuk, N. N. (1964). "Concerning Accuracy of Calendar Age in Processes of Normal and Pathological Aging." Leningrad Scientific-Research Institute of Labor Certification and of the Organization of the Work of Invalids, Leningrad.
Saunders, J. W., Jr. (1966). Science 154, 604.
Saunders, J. W., Jr. and Fallon, J. F. (1966). In "Major Problems in Developmental Biology" (M. Locke, ed.),

pp. 289-314, Academic Press, New York.

Siegel, J. S. and O'Leary, W. E. (1973). Current Population Reports, U. S. Bureau of the Census, Series P-23, No. 43, U. S. Government Printing Office, Washington.

Suzuki, Y. (1925). Mitt-Allg. Path. Sendai 2, 191.

Todaro, G. J. and Green, H. (1963). J. Cell.Biol. 17, 299.

Tomkins, G. A., Stanbridge, E. J. and Hayflick, L. (1974). Proc. Soc. Exp. Biol. Med. (in press).

Walford, R. L. (1969). "The Immunologic Theory of Aging." The Williams and Wilkins Co., Baltimore.

Whitten, J. M. (1969). Science 163, 1456.

CYCLING ⇄ NONCYCLING CELLS AS AN EXPLANATION FOR THE AGING PROCESS[1]

Seymour Gelfant, Ph.D.[2]
and
Gary L. Grove, Ph.D.[3]

Departments of Dermatology
and
Cell and Molecular Biology
Medical College of Georgia
Augusta, Georgia 30902

INTRODUCTION

In a recent report (Gelfant and Smith, 1972) we presented a model for cell and tissue aging. The model is based upon transitions of three categories of potentially proliferating cells. The first is cycling cells that are actively moving through the cell cycle, $G_1 \rightarrow S \rightarrow G_2 \rightarrow M$ (where G_1 and G_2 are gaps, S is the period of nuclear DNA synthesis, and M is the period of mitosis). The other two categories are noncycling cells, G_1-blocked and G_2-blocked, which are capable of moving into the cell cycle upon specific stimulation.

In this model (see figure 1) cellular aging is described as a progressive conversion of cycling to noncycling cells in tissues capable of proliferation. Noncycling cells become blocked either in the G_1 or the G_2 period of the cell cycle. They remain in these noncycling states until death or until they are recalled to proliferate in

---

[1]Supported by Research Grants AM16060, HD07745, and Training Grant AM05586 from the National Institutes of Health.
[2]Dr. Gelfant is Professor of Dermatology and Cell and Molecular Biology.
[3]Dr. Grove is Research Associate in the Department of Dermatology.

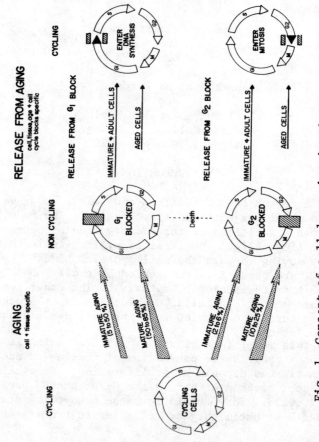

Fig. 1 Concept of cellular aging in tissues capable of proliferation. (Reproduced from Gelfant, S. and Smith, J. G., Jr. (1972), Science 178, 357.)

response to tissue injury or other proliferative stimuli. Some tissues complete their cellular aging transitions during embryogenesis (such as in pancreas, lens or tongue muscle) or before completion of maximum growth of the entire organism (for example, liver, kidney and bone); these tissues have undergone "immature aging" - in contrast to "mature aging" which takes place in other tissues during animal senescence (such as in epidermis and in epithelium of the gastrointestinal tract).

The transition of the noncycling state may be reversible; cells can be released from the G_1 and the G_2 blocks. This is depicted in figure 1 as release from aging. The degree and the rate of release may depend on whether cells are immature, adult, or chronologically aged, and on the particular tissue. Release from aging represents transition from the noncycling to the cycling state. The model also implies that released cycling cells may, in time, revert to noncycling states.

The present report provides two additional points of information in relation to our original concept (figure 1). The first is confirmatory and it deals with cellular aging transitions from cycling to noncycling states which occur in human fibroblasts in vitro. The second involves a dramatic in vivo example showing that the ability of non-cycling cells to be released to the cycling state diminishes with chronological age.

CYCLING $\longrightarrow$ NONCYCLING "AGING" TRANSITION IN VITRO

Hayflick (1974) has recently introduced the term "cytogerontology" to refer to that area of gerontological research dealing with studies of cultured cells (also see his chapter in present monograph). These studies, originally reported by Hayflick and Moorhead (1961) showed that normal animal cells cannot be maintained in vitro indefinitely, but rather have a limited life span. The life span is expressed in the proliferative capacity of the cells in culture and it is also directly related to the age of the donor from which the cultured cells were taken. The maximum life span of human diploid cells in vitro is about 10 months. This life span represents approximately 50 cell population doublings and it applies to cells taken from the youngest possible tissue, that is, from human fetal tissue. By comparison, shorter life spans and progressively fewer cell population doublings are observed in cultures originating from adult and old human tissues. These observations hold true only for normal, nontransformed diploid cells. (Human fibroblast-like cells that have unlimited life spans in vitro are abnormal, aneuploid cells with chromosomal anomalies.) The significance of the human diploid tissue culture lies in its similarity to normal cellular aging in vivo. Consequently, it provides a model system for studying both in vivo and in vitro aging of certain cell types.

The patterns of cell division of cultured cells undergoing aging in vitro coincide with, and can be explained by the four aging transitions depicted in figure 1. Merz and Ross (1969) observed individual cells throughout the life span of a human diploid culture derived from fetal lung tissue. They showed that the proportion of nondividing cells gradually increased from one to 48 percent with time in culture, thus providing evidence that cellular aging represents a general transition from the cycling to the noncycling state. The studies of Macieira-Coelho and associates (1966a, b; 1969; 1970) provide specific evidence for immature and mature aging transitions to both G_1- and G_2- blocked cells.

Using H^3-thymidine and autoradiography to demonstrate DNA synthesis, these investigators made detailed cell cycle analyses of both adult and embryonic human diploid cells during the various growth phases in vitro. They found that the decrease in proliferation associated with aging in vitro is due to cells becoming G_1-blocked (as shown by the decreased number of cells that take up H^3- thymidine, that is, synthesize DNA) and to cells becoming G_2-blocked (as shown by the decline in the number of cells that enter mitosis after DNA synthesis). Moreover, the relative percentages of cells that become G_1- or G_2-blocked and the fact that these transitions occur in both embryonic and in adult tissues substantiate the designations of immature and mature aging in figure 1. More recently, Cristofalo and Sharf (1973) have provided an accurate correlation between the percentage life span completed to the percentage of cells which will incorporate H^3-thymidine in WI-38 human diploid fibroblasts. As the percentage life span increases (i.e., cultures become older) the percentage of autoradiographically-labeled nuclei decreases -

108

emphasizing the transition from the cycling to the non-cycling state with aging _in vitro_. Their correlation reportedly is so accurate that it can be used to determine the "age" or passage level of stock cultures of human diploid cell lines.

Recently, microspectrocytophotometry has been used to characterize the cycling to noncycling transitions which occur as a function of _in vitro_ age. Cytophotometry, when used in conjunction with cytochemical procedures specific for DNA, allows one to measure nuclear DNA contents on an individual cell basis and it thus provides a tool by which cell cycle patterns can be studied. Figure 2 shows the relationship of nuclear DNA content to the periods of the cell cycle. In figure 2(B), 2C and 4C refer to diploid and tetraploid "classes" of DNA contents, according to the terminology introduced by Swift (1950).

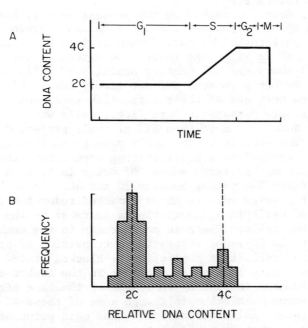

Fig. 2 Cytophotometric analysis of cell proliferation (A) Relationship of DNA content and cell cycle period, (B) DNA content profile.

(The corresponding terms 2N and 4N used by cytogeneticists refer to diploid and tetraploid "number" of chromosome sets.) As shown in figure 2(A), interphase cells in the G_1 period have a nuclear DNA content of 2C. During S, the DNA content gradually doubles. Cells in G_2 have a nuclear DNA content of 4C. During the visible stages of mitosis (M), chromosome DNA contents of prophase and metaphase cells are 4C and drop to 2C when the chromosomes separate during anaphase and telophase. Figure 2(B) presents a DNA content profile obtained by microspectrocytophotometric measurements of DNA contents in individual cell nuclei (this procedure is carried out in our laboratory using a Vickers M85 scanning microdensitometer and measuring Feulgen stained nuclei). Interphase cells in G_1 appear in the 2C mode of the histogram, while those in the G_2 period appear in the 4C mode. Cells in S have intermediate DNA values between 2C and 4C and they appear in the interclass range.

Dr. Grove, coauthor of the present report, has recently used this cytophotometric approach to determine proliferative patterns of cultured human diploid cells as a function of in vitro age (Grove and Mitchell, 1973). Figure 3 shows the DNA content profiles of cells in a "young" or early passage culture (i.e., cells which have completed only 40% of their total life span) and in an "old" or late passage culture (i.e., cells which have already completed more than 85% of their projected life span). The profile of the early passage culture is one which is typical of a proliferating population; the key feature being the large number of cells in S, as shown by intermediate DNA values between 2C and 4C. In contrast, the last passage culture shows a marked reduction in the number of cells in S, indicating a decrease in the number of cycling cells. There is an increase in the number of cells in the 2C mode, suggesting a transition of previously cycling cells to a noncycling G_1-blocked state. In addition, there is also an increase in the number of cells in the 4C mode indicating that some of the late passage cells become G_2-blocked (although some of these 4C cells may represent polyploidization). The main point of figure 3 is that it confirms the autoradiographic evidence (also see Yanishevsky et al., 1973) showing that cycling cells become noncycling G_1- and G_2-blocked cells throughout the life span of a human diploid cell culture. In addition,

110

figure 3 shows that the predominant transition is to the noncycling G_1-blocked state.

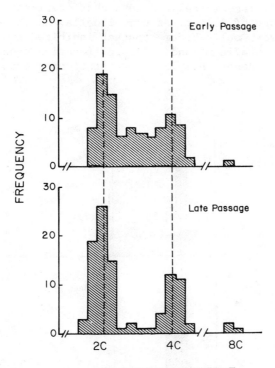

Fig. 3 DNA content profiles of human diploid fibro-blasts WI-38 in young (early passage) and in old (late passage) cultures.

Figure 4 shows the DNA content profiles during the log and the plateau growth phases of a subcultivated early passage culture of human diploid fibroblasts (a culture which had completed about 40% of its life span). During the log phase (36 hours after setting up the culture) the DNA content profile is typical of a proliferating popula-tion, showing a relatively large number of cells in S. In contrast, when the culture has reached the plateau phase,

111

120 hours after subcultivation, there is a decrease in the interclass values and a marked increase in the number of cells in the 2C mode. These results again illustrate a transition of cycling to noncycling G_1-blocked cells - which in this case is related to a characteristic culture growth feature of cultivated normal cells. As the cell density increases, cells become contact inhibited and the culture becomes confluent and cell proliferation ceases (i.e., the culture reaches the plateau or stationary phase).

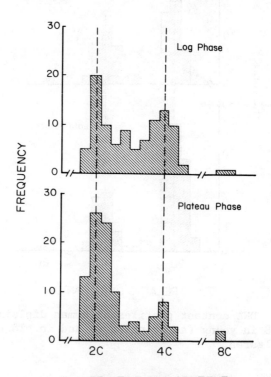

RELATIVE DNA CONTENT

Fig. 4 DNA content profiles of human diploid fibroblasts WI-38 during the log and plateau phases of growth of an early passage culture. (Adapted from Grove, G. L. and Mitchell, R. B. (1973), Proc. Penn. Acad. Sci. 47, 67.)

Westermark (1973) has recently made a detailed analysis of
this phenomenon in cultures of normal human glia-like
cells. His cytophotometric results are similar to those
on WI-38 fibroblasts (shown in figure 4). In addition,
Westermark demonstrates that when cell membrane movement
and cell locomotion are inhibited by cytochalasin B, cells
become blocked in the G_1 period - thus establishing an
important connection between cell membrane activities and
the control of cell proliferation. It should be pointed
out that there is a relationship between the number of
times that cells reach the plateau phase and their finite
life span in vitro. Since these culture growth changes
involve a transition of cycling to noncycling cells, they
may be viewed in terms of our model of cellular aging presented in figure 1.

IMPAIRED NONCYCLING $\longrightarrow$ CYCLING RELEASE
WITH CHRONOLOGICAL AGE IN VIVO

The second point to be taken up involves the release
of noncycling cells to the cycling state; this is designa-
ted as a release from (cellular) aging in figure 1.
Adelman and associates (1972) have provided a dramatic
example showing that the ability of noncycling cells to be
released to the cycling state is severely diminished with
chronological age. Some of their results are shown in
figure 5. Although the data in figure 5 relate to H^3-
thymidine incorporation into DNA as measured by specific
radioactivity extracted from parotid glands, they also
reflect cell proliferation of parotid gland cells, as observed by autoradiography and mitosis. Most of the parotid
gland cells in both 2-month-old and in 12-month-old rats
are noncycling (as shown by the low base line levels of
H^3-thymidine incorporation in figure 5). Following the
administration of isoproterenol to 2-month-old rats, the
degree of incorporation of H^3-thymidine into parotid
gland DNA is stimulated 70-fold. The increase in specific
radioactivity of DNA is initiated at 30 hours and reaches
a maximum 34 hours after isoproterenol injection. In
contrast, following administration of an identical body
weight dosage of isoproterenol to 12-month-old rats, the
time required to initiate the increase in specific radioactivity of DNA increases from 30 to 42 hours and the
magnitude of the response is inhibited approximately 70%.

113

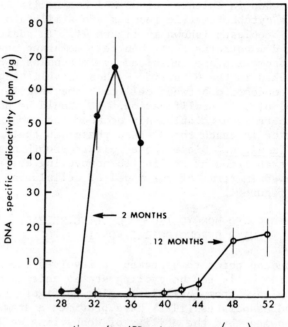

Fig. 5 Age-dependent loss of ability to incorporate H³-thymidine into rat parotid gland DNA after administration of isoproterenol. (Reproduced from Adelman, R. C., Stein, G., Roth, G. S. and Englander, D. (1972), Mechanisms of Ageing and Development 1, 49.)

In addition, the authors present evidence and indicate that cell proliferation is almost completely abolished in the parotid glands of 12-month-old rats treated with isoproterenol. This study strongly suggests that the capability of noncycling cells to be released to the cycling state may be impaired or even totally lost during chronological aging.

SUMMARY AND SIGNIFICANCE

In the present report, we have briefly reviewed our original concept of cellular aging as being due to

transitions of cycling to noncycling cells in tissues
capable of proliferation. We have provided additional
evidence for these noncycling "aging" transitions. We have
also presented information indicating that the capability
of reversible transition to the cycling state may be lost
with chronological age. In order for our ideas to play a
significant role in gerontological research, they should
be applicable to the age-related changes dealing with whole
animal senescence or mean life span. The most logical
system to which our ideas apply involves the age-related
decline of proliferative activity of cells in the immune
system. This field of research has been studied most
thoroughly and vigorously in recent years by Makinodan,
Perkins, and their associates (see references in Heidrick
and Makinodan, 1972; Hori et al., 1973; and Perkins and
Makinodan, in press). In addition, there is the impressive
immunological theory of aging presented by Walford (1969)
which attributes general senescence to immune dysfunction.

The studies of Makinodan, Perkins, and associates
investigating deficiencies of immunocompetent cells of
aged mice indicate that both the humoral and the cell-
mediated immune responses decline with advancing age. In
general, the humoral immune responses involve proliferation
and antibody formation by B-cell lymphocytes, whereas cell-
mediated immune responses such as delayed hypersensitivity,
tumor rejection and graft-versus-host reactions involve
proliferation of T-cell lymphocytes. In addition, there
is recent evidence that T-cell interaction is also involved
in antibody formation (see Heidrick and Makinodan, 1972).
Although the results shown in figure 6 deal with the proliferative capacity of mouse immunocompetent T-cells, they
also apply to mouse immunocompetent B-cell antibody forming
lymphocytes (Price and Makinodan, 1972).* The results in
figure 6 show clearly and dramatically that there is a
gradual and inevitable decline in proliferative activity
of mouse immunocompetent cells with age. It should be
pointed out that proliferation of immunocompetent cells is
determined experimentally by stimulating B-cells with antigens or T-cells in vitro with phytohemagglutinin. Since
most precursor immunocytes are in the noncycling state,
this decline in stimulated proliferative activity could
also represent a diminished ability of noncycling immunocompetent cells to be released to the cycling state with
chronological age (similar to the IPR-parotid gland results

discussed above).

The general decline in immunological surveillance that occurs with age can be related to reduced life span, to autoimmune disease and to overall senescence (Hori et al., 1973; Walford, 1969; and Perkins and Makinodan, in press). Since immunological surveillance depends upon proliferation of immunocompetent cells, our concept of explaining aging in terms of cycling⇄noncycling transitions, and particularly the evidence showing impaired release of noncycling cells to the cycling state with age, may be relevant in viewing the overall process of senescence in man.

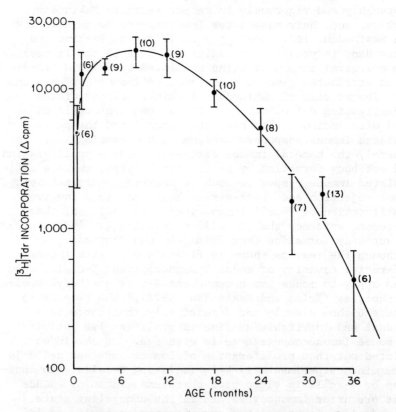

Fig. 6 Decrease in proliferative capacity of mouse immunocompetent T-cells with age. (Reproduced from Hori, Y., Perkins, E.H. and Halsall, M.K. (1973), Proc. Soc. Exp. Biol. Med. 144, 48.)

REFERENCES

Adelman, R. C., Stein, G., Roth, G. S. and Englander, D. (1972). Mechanisms of Ageing and Development 1, 49.

Cristofalo, V. J. and Sharf, B. B. (1973). Exp. Cell Res. 76, 419.

Gelfant, S. and Smith, J. G., Jr. (1972). Science 178, 357.

Grove, G. L. and Mitchell, R. B. (1973). Proc. Penn. Acad. Sci. 47, 67.

Hayflick, L. (1974). The Gerontologist 14, 37.

Hayflick, L. and Moorhead, P. S. (1961). Exp. Cell Res. 25, 585.

Heidrick, M. L. and Makinodan, T. (1972). Gerontologia 18, 305.

Hori, Y., Perkins, E. H. and Halsall, M. K. (1973). Proc. Soc. Exp. Biol. Med. 144, 48.

Macieira-Coelho, A. (1970). In "Aging in Cell and Tissue Culture" (E. Holečková and V. J. Cristofalo, eds.), pp. 121-132, Plenum, New York.

Macieira-Coelho, A. and Pontén, J. (1969). J. Cell Biol. 43, 374.

Macieira-Coelho, A., Pontén, J. and Philipson, L. (1966a). Exp. Cell Res. 42, 673.

Macieira-Coelho, A., Pontén, J. and Philipson, L. (1966b). Exp. Cell Res. 43, 20.

Merz, G. S. and Ross, J. D. (1969). J. Cell Physiol. 74, 219.

Perkins, E. H. and Makinodan, T. (1974). In "Proceedings of the First Rocky Mountain Symposium on Aging", Colorado State University, (in press).

Price, G. B. and Makinodan, T. (1972). J. Immunol. 108, 403.

Swift, H. H. (1950). Physiol. Zool. 23, 169.

Walford, R. L. (1969). "The Immunologic Theory of Aging." The Williams and Wilkins Co., Baltimore.

Westermark, B. (1973). Exp. Cell Res. 82, 341.

Yanishevesky, R., Mendelsohn, M. L., Mayall, B. H. and Cristofalo, V. J. (1973). In Vitro 8, 428.

---

*Addendum to page 115: Gerbase-DeLima, M., Wilkinson, J., Smith, G. S. and Walford, R. L. (1974). J. Gerontol. 29, 261.

PHYSIOLOGICAL THEORIES OF AGING

Nathan W. Shock, Ph.D.

Gerontology Research Center
National Institute of Child Health
and Human Development
National Institutes of Health
PHS, U.S. Department of Health,
Education and Welfare
Bethesda, Maryland
and the Baltimore City Hospitals
Baltimore, Maryland 21224

One of the problems of gerontology is that there are too many hypotheses and too few data to test them. Traditionally, many of the hypotheses about aging and senescence were not stated in terms which could be tested experimentally. In other instances the hypotheses as stated have required for testing analytical methods and techniques which were simply not available. With the rapid advances in molecular biology, protein chemistry, and immunology, new methods have been developed which are much more sensitive so that many hypotheses about the cellular basis of aging can now be restated in terms amenable to experimental tests. For example, we are now in a position to make the critical tests of the error hypothesis, which assumes that aging results from the accumulation of errors in the transmission of information from the DNA molecule to the final protein product. Methods are now available which will permit the isolation and identification of proteins which are different and hence, presumably, either inactive or inefficient in their performance of intracellular reactions.

Some hypotheses focus attention on alterations in the DNA molecule itself. Among these, radiation effects, "wear and tear" damage to the DNA molecule itself, as well as the role of histones and non-histone proteins in influencing the read-out of the DNA molecule may be

mentioned. Although Curtis and Crowley (1963) have reported an increased incidence of atypical chromosomes in the
liver from animals exposed to radiation, altered DNA
molecules have not been isolated. It has also been shown
that histones are more tightly bound to DNA in tissue from
old animals than in young (von Hahn et al., 1969), but the
biological effects of this binding have not yet been
identified. Mechanisms for the repair of DNA have also
been reported, but the question of whether damaged DNA
accumulates in aged tissues has not been resolved. Since
the incidence of mutations does not increase markedly with
increasing age of parents, it is believed that the DNA
molecule is very stable, so that age changes do not seem
very likely.

From the standpoint of molecular biology, the introduction of errors in the transmission of information from
the DNA to the final protein product seems a more likely
basis for aging than changes in the DNA molecule itself
(Medvedev, 1961, 1964, 1966). Experimental tests of these
possibilities depend on the ability to detect intermediary
products, such as atypical RNAs and their products at
specific points in the chain of events. Similarly,
hypotheses involving the formation of cross-links in
specific proteins (Bjorksten, 1968; Sinex, 1964) and the
formation of free radicals (Harman, 1956, 1962) require
the detection and isolation of specific molecular species
if they are to be tested experimentally.

Although this error hypothesis of aging is an
attractive one, it must be remembered that many of the
details of the molecular events which occur are still un-
certain and much work in cellular biology remains to be
done. Much of the current theory is based on evidence
derived from studies on bacterial systems and many critical
questions are still unanswered, especially with respect to
mammalian cells. Recent developments in the techniques
of cell fusion, coupled with the ability to culture these
cells, provide a unique opportunity to differentiate
between genetic and cytoplasmic factors in cellular aging.
Radio-immunoassay techniques also permit identification
of minute amounts of any atypical protein that may be
formed which must then be isolated and subjected to amino
acid sequencing. In my opinion, if these new methods are
vigorously applied in the field of gerontology we should
within the next few years have data necessary to test

these hypotheses which are concerned with aging at the cellular level.

There is, however, still a large gap between cell biology and aging or performance in a total animal. With the possible exception of the autoimmune theory, none of these hypotheses deal with possible interactions among cells or the possible role of physiological control mechanisms which are important in maintaining the integrity of the total animal. It is, therefore, important to give consideration to physiological theories which may explain what happens with aging in the total animal.

One such hypothesis is the autoimmune theory of aging (Blumenthal and Berns, 1964; Walford, 1964). Since this hypothesis has been discussed by a previous speaker in this symposium, it will not be reviewed here.

The wear and tear theory of aging has a long history and popular appeal (Sacher, 1966). As the name implies, the theory assumes that an organism "wears out" with use much like inanimate objects. However, the man-machine analogy fails to take into account two important characteristics of an organism which do not apply to machines. In the first place, a living organism is endowed with a multitude of mechanisms for self-repair which are not available to a machine, and, secondly, functions in an organism may actually be improved by use. One example is the results of physical exercise and training on muscle strength, as for example, the hypertrophied muscles of the weight lifter and the improved cardiovascular performance observed in the trained athlete.

The wear and tear theory gained its greatest support from observations that increasing the environmental temperature of poikilothermic animals significantly shortens life span (Loeb and Northrup, 1917). The argument was that with an increase in temperature there was an associated increase in the rate of metabolism in the animal which accelerated the rate at which it would wear out. It should be pointed out, however, that the observed life shortening effect of increased temperatures could also be used as evidence for increased rate of biochemical changes in the animal, such as the rate at which cross-links could be formed. The data, therefore, are not unique to the wear and tear theory.

Carlson et al. (1957) as well as Johnson et al. (1961) conducted experiments which tend to indicate that increasing the metabolic rate in a warm-blooded animal will reduce its life span. In these experiments, rats were kept throughout most of their life spans at quite cold temperatures so that the animals had to increase their metabolism by about 30% in order to maintain their body temperature. The rats did not die of respiratory infections but all causes of death were represented, including the occurrence of cancers. These experiments give some credence to the rate of living or wear and tear theory, but it must be remembered that exposure to cold has widespread physiological effects in addition to the increase in metabolic rate.

Pearl (1928) assumed that men engaged in heavy work throughout their lifetime were subjected to a greater degree of wear and tear than those who engaged in light work. On the basis of this assumption he compared death rates of various labor groups in England and Wales. The workers were divided into five groups according to the degree of physical labor involved in their work. Group I engaged in very light work, Group V in very heavy labor. He concluded that death rates were roughly independent of the degree of labor up to age 45, but that after that age, there was increased mortality among workers engaged in very heavy labor (Table I). In order to support the wear and tear theory there should be a progressive rise in death rates from Group I to V. However, examination of the table does not show such a progression in mortality at any age.

TABLE I

MEAN DEATH RATES PER 1000 AT THE AGES INDICATED FOR OUTDOOR WORKERS IN THE LABOR CATEGORIES INDICATED (FROM PEARL, 1924)

Labor group	Age group						65-74	75 and Over
	15-19	20-24	25-34	35-44	45-54	55-64		
I	1.27	2.45	3.57	6.02	11.29	23.49	52.58	163.00
II	1.63	3.16	4.05	7.38	13.97	29.30	67.62	174.93
III	1.29	2.97	4.51	6.34	11.64	23.88	56.39	162.20
IV	1.46	2.60	3.61	6.17	10.77	22.70	52.91	177.25
V	1.83	2.64	3.44	6.21	12.71	29.31	77.37	211.07

In fact, the mortality rate for Group IV laborers, aged 55 to 64, was actually the lowest of any labor group. About the best that can be said for the data is that over age 55 heavy laborers have a higher mortality rate than those who carry out only light work. Furthermore, studies on humans are extremely difficult to interpret since those who are engaged in heavy labor in all probability were selected from lower socio-economic groups where income, housing, and general living conditions, as well as access to medical care, were not doubt less than optimal.

In experiments on animals, Selye (1966) has identified three stages of responses to continued exposure to a variety of stresses, namely: 1) The alarm reaction in which adaptive forces (endocrine, nervous) are being activated but are not yet fully operational, 2) the stage of resistance in which mobilization of the defensive reactions is completed, and 3) the stage of exhaustion, which eventually terminates in a breakdown of resistance and death.

Selye regards these three phases of response to stress as reminiscent of three phases of aging: 1) Childhood in which adaptability is great but adaptation is still limited, 2) adulthood during which the body has acquired resistance to most agents likely to affect it in life, and 3) senescence with its characteristic exhaustion of resistance that is conducive to death.

He has also reported experiments with rats which indicate an increased sensitivity to stresses in animals which have been forced to adapt to uninterrupted treatment with damaging agents, such as lowered environmental temperature, forced muscular exercise, drugs, or hormones. It is claimed that most stresses leave some residual deficit and that aging is the result of the accumulation of these small residual damages, which may be so small that they cannot be detected individually.

While it is true that the old animal has a marked reduction in ability to withstand stress and will succumb to a stress which can be tolerated by a young animal, there is no proof that repeated stresses are the cause of aging. Although Selye's work has been very important in showing relationship between stress and disease, it has not shed much light on the mechanisms of aging.

Curtis and his coworkers have provided experimental evidence that repeated stresses induced by tetanus toxin or tetanus toxoid did not significantly shorten life span

123

of mice (figure 1). In these experiments (Curtis and Gebhard, 1958), doses of tetanus toxoid and tetanus toxin were given every 14 days to two groups of mice, with a control group receiving saline injections. Since the mice developed an immunity to the toxin, another group of mice was treated the same way as the experimental group in each case. Each time before an experimental group was injected, a small sample from the other group was used to determine the LD_{50} dose of the toxin at that time. The experimental group was then given half of this dose. In this way the mice received a severe stress at each injection. The stress was continued for almost a year. There was no effect on subsequent mortality from these repeated doses of tetanus toxin or toxoid.

SURVIVAL FOR MICE GIVEN SUBCUTANEOUS INJECTIONS
EVERY 14 DAYS OF TETANUS TOXIN OR
TETANUS TOXOID

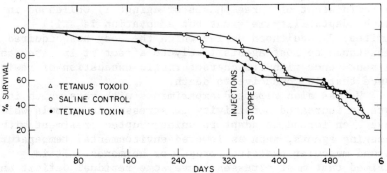

Fig. 1 Survival curves for mice receiving large but non-fatal doses every 14 days of the agents indicated for a large fraction of their life spans. These severe stresses did not alter the life expectancy of the animals after the treatments were stopped. (From: Curtis, H. J. and Gebhard, K. L., 1958).

Similar results were obtained when the mice were given subcutaneous injections of sterile turpentine which formed large sterile ulcers which gradually broke down to form large open sores (Curtis and Gebhard, 1960). As soon

as the mouse had recovered, another sterile ulcer was formed in another area. After one year, the injections were
stopped and it was found that life expectancy of these mice
was the same as that of the controls.

These experiments indicate quite clearly that a general large stress _per se_, even though it is repeated often
over a long period of time, does not cause the deterioration characteristic of senescence. It does not seem that
the accumulation of stresses is the cause of senescence in
the normal animal.

For completeness, the hypoxia theory of aging should
be mentioned (McFarland, 1963). According to this theory,
aging is primarily a result of lowered oxygen tension,
especially in critical areas such as the brain. Support
for the hypoxia theory of aging comes largely from the
similarity of changes in psychomotor performance, such as
handwriting in older people, which can be induced in young
subjects under conditions of lowered oxygen tension of
inspired air. However, there is little experimental evidence to support this hypothesis. Oxygen tension of the
blood remains uniform even into advanced old age and although there may be a slight fall in oxygen saturation of
arterial blood, it does not seem to be large enough to
induce a significant lowering of oxygen tensions at the
tissue level. Furthermore, studies of isolated tissues
have thus far failed to demonstrate any significant decrement in oxygen uptake when calculated on the basis of cell
numbers.

Kohn (1971) has attempted to relate the age change in
collagen to changes in other physiological systems with
age. Starting with the observed information that collagen
becomes stiffer with age, Kohn believes that, since
collagen constitutes 25 to 30 percent of the total body
protein and is distributed in and around blood vessels and
cells, its change in properties may influence other physiological functions. According to this hypothesis, the reduced performance of cardiac muscle is ascribed to increasing stiffness. Large arteries would be less able to transmit contractile force. Connective tissue changes in small
blood vessels may lead to the development of hypertension.
Since the passage of materials between blood vessel and
cell takes place through a collagen containing matrix,
changes in collagen may interfere with diffusion processes,
resulting in impairments in function even at the cellular

level. As Kohn has pointed out, this is a highly specula-
tive hypothesis.

Furthermore, chemical agents which interfere with the
maturation of collagen and the formation of cross-links
should increase life span. However, experiments in which
rats have been treated with such substances (nitriles and
penicilamine) have failed to produce an increase in life
span. It is, therefore, doubtful whether this hypothesis
can explain aging in the total animal.

In the past, physiological theories about aging have
been highly specific and in general have focused on the
endocrine system. For example, the presumption that in-
ability of the sex glands to secrete adequate amounts of
hormone led to the injection of testicular extracts and
the transplantation of gonads as a "cure for aging" in the
earlier part of this century (McGrady, 1968). Similarly,
the assumption that aging was the result of general slowing
of cellular metabolism led to the proposal that aging was
primarily a result of impairment of the thyroid gland. As
knowledge about endocrinology advanced and the primary
role of the pituitary in regulating other endocrine glands
became apparent, failure of the pituitary gland was postulated as a primary cause of aging. However, it is now
apparent that none of these hypotheses is tenable as a
basic cause of aging. Furthermore, each hypothesis was
much too specific and could only deal with a limited set
of observations.

From a physiological standpoint it now seems that
aging must be regarded as a breakdown or impairment of
performance of endocrine and neural control mechanisms.
At the present state of knowledge, it would be premature
to propose this as a hypothesis to explain aging in the
total animal. However, it is useful to examine some data
which are beginning to point in this direction.

In the first place, when we examine data which have
been collected at the Gerontology Research Center over a
good many years, it appears that in humans, age decrements
are greater in performances which involve the coordinated
activities of a number of organ systems than in performances which are related to a single organ or tissue. For
example, figure 2 compares the age decrement in nerve
conduction velocity (Norris et al., 1953), creatinine
clearance (Rowe et al., 1974), cardiac output (Brandfonbrener et al., 1955), and maximum breathing capacity

(Norris et al., 1956) in males. In this chart, the average
value for 20-30-year-olds is taken as 100% and values for
subsequent decades are plotted as percentage of this value.
It may be seen that the age decrement for nerve conduction
velocity is considerably less than that for the maximum
breathing capacity. Measurements of nerve conduction
velocity are related to a single physiological system
whereas maximum breathing capacity involves the coordinated
activity of the nervous and muscular systems. Creatinine
clearance and cardiac output involve a broad spectrum of
control mechanisms which are closely regulated but are not
as highly dependent upon coordinated activity as is maximum
breathing capacity.

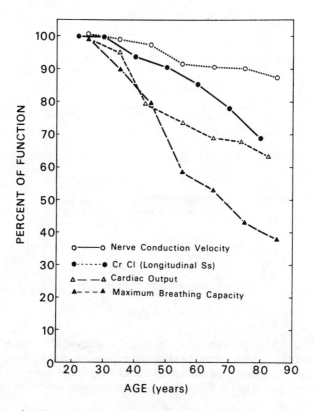

Fig. 2 Percentage decrements in selected physiological functions. (Cr Cl = creatinine clearance.)

Figure 3 compares on the same basis age decrements in muscle strength with the maximum power generated by the same muscle groups used in cranking an ergometer (Shock and Norris, 1970). It is apparent that the coordinated performance (cranking) shows a greater age decrement than the static strength of the same muscle groups.

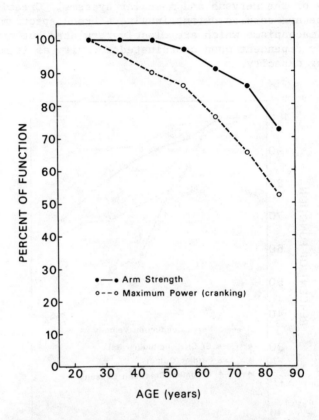

Fig. 3   Age decrements in muscle strength (●—●) compared with decrements in maximum powers developed in a coordinated movement (cranking)utilizing the same muscle groups (o—o).   (Data from Shock, N. W. and Norris, A. H., 1970.)

It has also been shown that age decrements increase
as the complexity of the task increases (Birren, 1965;
Welford, 1965). For example, simple reflex time does not
change significantly over the entire age span of 20-80
years (Hügin et al., 1960). This response which operates
primarily through the spinal cord involves transmission of
nerve impulses over short distances and through a relatively few synapses. In contrast, reaction time, which
involves transmission through many synapses as well as
influences of other factors in the central nervous system,
shows significant decrements with age. Furthermore, when
choice reaction times are measured age differences are
even greater. In fact, there is a linear relationship
between reaction times and the amount of stimulus information in both young and old (Suci et al., 1960) (figure 4).
The fact that the slope of the regression curve of reaction
time on stimulus information is greater for the old subjects than for the young indicates the effect of age on
increasing the time required for the response.

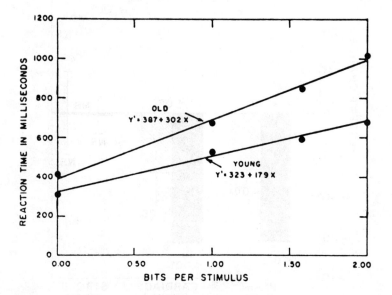

Fig. 4 Reaction time as a function of stimulus
information and age. (From: Suci, G. J., Davidoff, M. D.,
and Surwillo, W. W., 1960.)

It has also been shown that the effectiveness of one of the mechanisms involved in the control of heart rate is less effective in the old than in the young (Rothbaum et al., 1974). In these experiments, blood pressure was increased by 50 millimeters in both old and young unanesthetized rats by the continuous infusion of phenylephrine. The response to this stimulus, namely, the lowering of the heart rate, was significantly less in the senescent than in the young animals (figure 5). These experiments indicate a reduction in the effectiveness of a physiological control mechanism with increasing age.

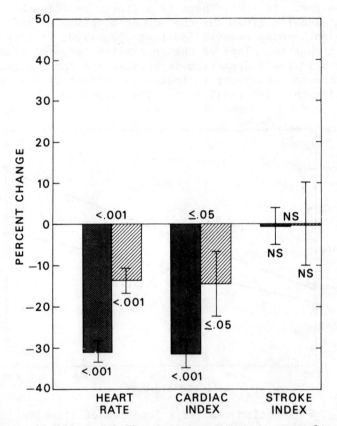

Fig. 5 Effect of 50 mm Hg increment in systolic blood pressure on heart rate, cardiac index, and stroke index in old and young unanesthetized rats.

130

Other evidence of impaired control mechanisms in the aged is offered by the reduced ability to adjust to alterations in environmental temperatures. For example, exposures to ambient temperatures of 5 to 15 degrees for 45 to 120 minutes produced insignificant changes in rectal temperature in young subjects whereas aged subjects showed a fall of 0.5 to 1 degree C (Krag and Kountz, 1950, 1952). Aged subjects also showed an impairment in the ability to adjust to increase in environmental temperature. The death rate from heat stroke rises sharply after the age of 60. Shattuck and Hilferty (1932) found an increase from 8 per 100,000 deaths between the ages of 70 and 79 to 80 per 100,000 deaths for ages 90 to 100 years.

Experimental studies also indicate a slower rate of adaptation to heat stress in the aged than in the young. In studies on the maximum rate of heat elimination from the hand, Pickering (1936) found that under standard conditions the heat output in calories per minute per unit volume was approximately 33% lower at age 70 than at age 25. In senile subjects the rate of water loss from the surface of the finger tip and toe was also significantly lower in the aged than in the young subjects, thus reducing the potential heat loss from evaporation (Burch et al., 1942).

A number of examples of the breakdown of endocrine control mechanisms in the aged can be cited. For example, the response of the kidney to a standard amount of antidiuretic hormone is significantly less in the aged subject than in the young (Miller and Shock, 1953) (figure 6). In these experiments measurements of the U/P ratio of inulin were made in young, middle aged, and old subjects following the infusion of a standard dose of pitressin. The response as measured by the increase in U/P ratio of inulin was significantly less in both the senescent and the middle aged subjects than in the young.

The age-associated reduction in glucose tolerance (Silverstone et al., 1957) can also be explained on the basis of a reduction in the sensitivity of the beta cells of the pancreas to the blood sugar level (Shock and Andres, 1968). Dr. Andres and his associates have carried out extensive experiments in which the amount of insulin released can be determined at specific blood glucose levels. These experiments involve a technique in which the rate of glucose infusion is adjusted to give a stable blood sugar

level which can be determined by the experimenter (Andres
et al., 1965). Other experiments have been conducted
showing that there is no age difference in the peripheral
utilization of glucose (Andres et al., 1969). Consequently
the age difference in insulin release at specific blood
sugar levels, as shown in figure 7, can be attributed to
lowered sensitivity of beta cells of the pancreas to a
given level of blood sugar in the aged.

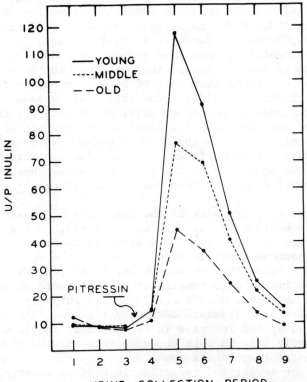

Fig. 6 Mean values of U/P inulin ratio for each of
three age groups before and after the intravenous administration of pitressin. Urine collection periods 1-9 represent nine consecutive 12-minute periods. Pitressin was administered immediately after the conclusion of period 3.
(From: Miller, J. H. and Shock, N. W., 1953.)

EFFECT OF AGE ON GLUCOSE-INSULIN RESPONSE CURVE

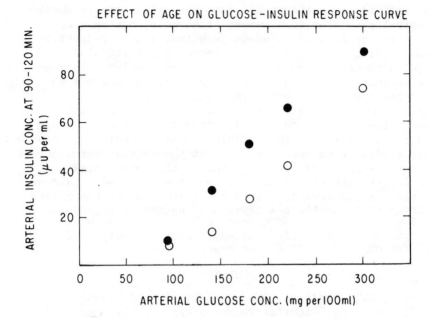

Fig. 7 Effect of age on insulin blood levels at
specified blood glucose concentrations in young (•) and
old (o) subjects.

There is also considerable evidence that the primary
age deficit in the physiological responses to hormone
stimulation lies in the sensitivity of the target organ.
In many instances the target organs are capable of responding when an adequate stimulus is provided. For example,
the experimental administration of TSH produced the same
elevation of oxygen consumption, increase in I^{131} uptake
of the thyroid gland, and increase of PBI in the blood in
old and young subjects (Baker et al., 1959). These experiments indicate that the thyroid gland in the aged is capable of responding to the physiological stimulus. Similarly the physiological responses to the administration of
ACTH and cortisone were essentially similar in old and
young subjects (Duncan et al., 1952). The administration
of exogenous estrogen and progesterone can stimulate
endometrial bleeding in post-menopausal women (Masters and

Allen, 1948). From these and similar experiments it may
be inferred that the significant age difference in physiological responses to a number of hormones may be a reflection of the lack of an adequate stimulus or a reduction in
the sensitivity of the target organ to the stimulus.

Although the evidence is far from complete, it seems
to me that further investigations should be focused on the
general hypothesis that aging, at least in the total
animal, may be a reflection of the breakdown of control
mechanisms. Although I would agree that the basic cause
of aging may lie at the cellular level, I would urge consideration of perhaps less elegant theoretical formulations
directed toward explaining aging in the total animal. We
no longer expect to find a general overall theory that will
explain all diseases. Similarly, I doubt whether a single
theory will explain all aspects of aging. I believe that
aging should be looked upon as a highly complex phenomenon
which may require different explanatory principles for
different aspects of the process.

REFERENCES

Andres, R., Swerdloff, R., Pozefsky, T. and Coleman, D.
(1965). In "Chemical Pharmacology" (L. T. Skeggs, Jr.,
ed.), pp. 486-491, Mediad, Inc., New York.

Andres, R., Swerdloff, R. and Tobin, J. D. (1969). In
"Proceedings of the 8th International Congress of
Gerontology", Vol. I, pp. 36-39, Federation of American
Societies for Experimental Biology, Bethesda, Maryland.

Baker, S. P., Gaffney, G. W., Shock, N. W. and Landowne,
M. (1959). J. Gerontol. 14, 37.

Birren, J. E. (1965). In "Behavior, Aging, and the
Nervous System" (A. T. Welford and J. E. Birren, eds.),
pp. 191-216, Charles C. Thomas, Springfield, Illinois.

Bjorksten, J. (1968). J. Am. Geriat. Soc. 16, 408.

Blumenthal, H. T. and Berns, A. W. (1964). In "Advances
in Gerontological Research" (B. L. Strehler, ed.), Vol.
1, pp. 289-342, Academic Press, New York.

Brandfonbrener, M., Landowne, M. and Shock, N. W. (1955).
Circulation 12, 557.

Burch, G. E., Cohn, A. E. and Neumann, C. (1942). Am.
Heart J. 23, 185.

Carlson, L. D., Scheyer, W. J. and Jackson, H. B. (1957).
Radiation Res. 7, 190.

Curtis, H. J. and Crowley, C. (1963). Radiation Res. 19,

337.

Curtis, H. J. and Gebhard, K. L. (1958). In "Proceedings of the 2nd UN International Conference on Peaceful Uses of Atomic Energy", Vol. 22, "Biological Effects of Radiation", pp. 53-57, United Nations, New York.

Curtis, H. J. and Gebhard, K. L. (1960). In "The Biology of Aging" (B. L. Strehler, ed.), pp. 162-166, American Institute of Biological Sciences, Washington, D. C.

Duncan, L. E., Solomon, D. H., Rosenberg, E. K., Nichols, M. P. and Shock, N. W. (1952). J. Gerontol. 7, 351.

Harman, D. (1956). J. Gerontol. 11, 298.

Harman, D. (1962). Radiation Res. 16, 753.

Hügin, F., Norris, A. H. and Shock, N. W. (1960). J. Gerontol. 15, 388.

Johnson, H. D., Kintner, L. D. and Kibler, H. H. (1961). J. Gerontol. 18, 29.

Kohn, R. R. (1971). "Principles of Mammalian Aging." Prentice-Hall, Engelwood Cliffs, New Jersey.

Krag, C. L. and Kountz, W. B. (1950). J. Gerontol. 5, 227.

Krag, C. L. and Kountz, W. B. (1952). J. Gerontol. 7, 61.

Loeb, J. and Northrop, J. H. (1917). J. Biol. Chem. 32, 103.

Masters, W. H. and Allen, W. M. (1948). J. Gerontol. 3, 183.

McFarland, R. A. (1963). Ergonomics 6, 339.

McGrady, P. M., Jr. (1968). "The Youth Doctors." Coward-McCann, New York.

Medvedev, Z. A. (1961). Advances in Contemporary Biology 51, 299.

Medvedev, Z. A. (1964). In "Advances in Gerontological Research" (B. L. Strehler, ed.), Vol. 1, pp. 181-206, Academic Press, New York.

Medvedev, Z. A. (1966). "Protein Biosynthesis and Problems of Heredity, Development, and Aging." Oliver & Boyd, Edinburgh.

Miller, J. H. and Shock, N. W. (1953). J. Gerontol. 8, 446.

Norris, A. H., Shock, N. W. and Wagman, I. H. (1953). J. Appl. Physiol. 5, 589.

Norris, A. H., Shock, N. W., Landowne, M. and Falzone, J. A., Jr. (1956). J. Gerontol. 11, 379.

Pearl, R. (1928). "The Rate of Living: Being an Account of Some Experimental Studies on the Biology of Life Duration." A. A. Knopf, New York.

Pickering, G. W. (1936). Clin. Sci. 2, 209.

Rothbaum, D. A., Shaw, D. J., Angell, C. S. and Shock, N. W. (1974). J. Gerontol. (in press).

Rowe, J. W., Andres, R., Tobin, J. D., Norris, A. H. and Shock, N. W. (1974). Submitted for publication.

Sacher, G. A. (1966). In "Perspectives in Experimental Gerontology" (N. W. Shock, ed.), pp. 326-335, Charles C. Thomas, Springfield, Illinois.

Selye, H. (1966). In "Perspectives in Experimental Gerontology" (N. W. Shock, ed.), pp. 375-385, Charles C. Thomas, Springfield, Illinois.

Shattuck, G. C. and Hilferty, M. M. (1932). Am. J. Tropical Med. 12, 223.

Shock, N. W. and Andres, R. (1968). In "Adaptive Capacities of an Aging Organism" (D. F. Chebotarev, ed.), pp. 235-254, Acad. Sci., USSR, Kiev.

Shock, N. W. and Norris, A. H. (1970). In "Medicine and Sport", Vol. 4, "Physical Activity and Aging" (D. Brunner and E. Jokl, eds.), pp. 92-99, S. Karger, Basel.

Silverstone, F. A., Brandfonbrener, M., Shock, N. W. and Yiengst, M. J. (1957). J. Clin. Invest. 36, 504.

Sinex, F. M. (1964). In "Advances in Gerontological Research" (B. L. Strehler, ed.), Vol. 1, pp. 165-178, Academic Press, New York.

Suci, G. J., Davidoff, M. D. and Surwillo, W. W. (1960). J. Exp. Psychol. 60, 242.

von Hahn, H. P., Miller, J. and Eichhorn, G. L. (1969). Gerontologia 15, 293.

Walford, R. L. (1964). Exp. Gerontol. 1, 67.

Welford, A. T. (1965). In "Behavior, Aging, and the Nervous System" (A. T. Welford and J. E. Birren, eds.), pp. 3-20, Charles C. Thomas, Springfield, Illinois.

THE STUDY OF AGING IN MAN:
PRACTICAL AND THEORETICAL PROBLEMS

Reubin Andres, M. D.

Chief, Clinical Physiology Branch
Gerontology Research Center
National Institute of Child Health and Human Development
National Institutes of Health
at
The Baltimore City Hospitals
Baltimore, Maryland 21224

"The proper study of Man is Man, says Man."

. . . James Thurber

It was with a sense of relief that I heard the announcement at this meeting that the theme of the entire aging symposium next year would likely be "Aging in Man". This announcement frees me from the compulsion to attempt to be all-inclusive in my brief presentation this year. I intend therefore to be quite selective. I will review a few of the problems that are peculiar to the study of man, I will illustrate with one or two specific variables that we have been interested in, and I will discuss the statistical complexities and implications of attempts to define the _rate_ of aging of various processes in man.

In thinking about the unique problems involved in the study of man, one can come up with an impressive list of difficulties. The recent death of Samuel Goldwyn calls to mind one of his deathless aphorisms: "Anyone who goes to see a psychiatrist should have his head examined." The theme of this section could be a paraphrase of Goldwyn: "Anyone who undertakes the study of aging with man as his experimental animal should have his head examined."

1. Man is of course a genetic mish-mash. Brother-
sister multi-generational matings are frowned upon. An
important experimental control available to the biologist
is thus denied to the clinical investigator. The increased
utilization of twins in aging research would be helpful in
this regard, but such studies are obviously difficult.

2. Environmental diversity in man is immense and,
furthermore, is continually changing. Consider eating
habits as an obvious example. There is little difficulty
in feeding a large colony of rats the same nutrients over
their entire life span. A group of human subjects might
have dietary standardization imposed upon them for a few
days (again, with difficulty) but it is inconceivable that
a cohort could be selected at birth and maintained for
three score years and ten on identical diets. Furthermore,
the food intake in infancy and childhood of a group of
25-year olds today was quite different from that of their
50-year-old fathers or of their 75-year-old grandfathers.
These environmental differences undoubtedly influence aging
processes in important ways. The cross-sectional comparison of age groups reveals differences which are not necessarily due to biological aging processes per se, but may
also reflect these uncontrolled and, in many respects,
unknown environmental differences.

3. There are limitations on research procedures in
clinical investigation which necessarily hinder aging
studies. Subjects would be loathe to donate their thymuses
or their epididymal fat pads in the service of science.
One of the challenges to the clinical gerontologist, therefore, is the design of experiments which will not only
assess organ function but will also probe into the mechanism of age differences--and will do all this in the relatively undisturbed total animal preparation.

4. Another layer of difficulty in human research is
that of the necessity to obtain truly informed consent. The
principle has been so shabbily treated in certain instances
in the past that we are now faced with a swinging pendulum
which may seriously hamper essential research. The increasing realization by gerontologists that aging does not
miraculously start at the 21st birthday leads to the even
more complex issues of informed consent in minors. These

problems are under intensive scrutiny at this time.

     5. The inordinate <u>length of human life</u> is itself a
problem. Longitudinal life-span studies may very well
continue beyond the life of the investigator. There are
ingenious research strategies which have been devised in
an attempt to reduce the magnitude of this problem. Still,
the remarkable changes that take place as a rat ages from
3 months to 12, 18 and 24 months can be matched in man only
over a 70 year span of time. Physiological aging can be
easily detected in rats followed over a three- or six-month
period of time; I shall discuss the time needed to detect
age changes in man later in the discussion.
           Another way of thinking about the impact of man's
longevity is to consider that today's 80-year-old was a
child in the 1890's, 50-year olds grew up in the 1920's,
and 20-year olds in the 1950's. Contrast this to today's
senior rat who grew up in 1972.

     6. The problems of <u>population sampling</u> is also much
more serious for human studies than for animal studies.
Will a study of aging in upper-middle socio-economic class
males in Baltimore yield data which will be applicable to
aging processes in lower socio-economic class women in
Baluchistan? For that matter, will study of aging in the
impeccably overfed laboratory rat be applicable to the
foraging Egyptian sand-rat? There is a tacit assumption
that biologic studies will uncover biologic truths that
cross strain and species barriers. I don't mean to seem
paranoid about this, but it strikes me that when a new
mouse study turns up findings that show it to be different
from a previously reported rabbit study, no one accuses the
rabbit-investigator of shoddy experimental design for not
including mice among his subjects. In some human studies,
the investigator is likely to be severely reprimanded when
his subjects are found not to be a random sampling of <u>Homo
sapiens</u> on Mother Earth. I have unconscionably overstated
the problem and do not want to leave the impression that
meticulous attention to subject selection is not critical.
For some studies, however, certain design features of the
study make it necessary to compromise on matters of ran-
domized subject selection. I am reminded of an unkind
critic of a new Broadway play who derisively commented that
the play dealt with a true cross-section of humanity: a

priest, a prostitute, and a paraplegic.

7.   The interaction of aging and disease has been
generally considered to be a problem more or less unique
to clinical gerontology. I prefer to think that the sub-
tleties are just better dealt with in human research.
    We have, for example, chosen to study age differ-
ences in carbohydrate metabolism, renal function, and pulmonary function in man. We emphasize that our interest
(at one level of study, at least) is in defining true aging
of these physiological processes. We laboriously repeated-
ly measure (a) glucose tolerance, (b) 24-hour creatinine
clearance, and (c) maximum breathing capacity, as indices
of function of these systems. Now suppose that, as the
years go by, certain clinical events occur--and let us deal
with actual examples: (a) One group of subjects is placed
on antihypertensive medication which, in turn, has a deteriorative effect on glucose tolerance; another subject develops pancreatitis and knocks out a considerable fraction
of his insulin-producing beta cells; (b) Another group of
subjects develops urinary tract infections, others form
renal stones, and one even has a kidney removed after it is
injured in a motorcycle accident; (c) Still another group
of subjects develops chronic obstructive pulmonary disease,
and one develops bronchogenic carcinoma and has a lung removed.
    These diverse events, some chronic and perhaps
subtle, others acute and drastic in their impact on function, can be dealt with in two ways. One is the do-nothing
or the ostrich approach. The rationale for this approach is
roughly as follows: with increasing age there is an increased likelihood of developing a variety of diseases,
including (to stay with our examples) hypertension,
pyelonephritis, and carcinomas. In fact, with the passage
of time, i.e., with aging, there is an increased likelihood
of falling off a motorcycle. Therefore, all of these
events represent aging processes and part of the deterioration of function with aging is due to these age-related
diseases and accidents.
    The second approach can be rationalized as
follows: Suppose one has been monitoring the variables
listed over a period of years and has defined a gradual
progressive loss of function in each of them. Suddenly,
on the next visit, renal and pulmonary functions drop to

140

only half of what they had been on the previous visit since a kidney and a lung have been removed. The first approach would dictate: "Recompute the slopes; your subjects have aged in the interim." The second approach would dictate: "Clean up your data--code these events as diseases and do not include these or any further data points on these subjects in your estimates of the rate of aging of these systems." Since I labelled the first approach as the ostrich technique, clearly I favor the second method.

Now this "clinical purification" of the data is generally not believed to be necessary in animal research. Rats are selected which appear to be in reasonably good health. Strange things do happen however in animal colonies. In the historical experience of our own rat colonies, for example, we have seen periods when many of the older animals showed pulmonary infections and other times when glomerulonephritis became a problem.

8. Thus, while the disease vs. age dilemma is not unique to studies in man, the no-show, no-return, or drop-out problem is. Rats are not given the option of cancelling appointments; human volunteers may, for a variety of reasons, leave us. Interpretive problems in data handling can be quite difficult and serious. There are, however, techniques for assessing the impact of this complication. For example, suppose that of a series of 1,000 subjects examined for the first time in a longitudinal study of aging, 50 fail to return for subsequent visits. Those 50 can be compared with the 950 who remained faithful. Were there differences already evident in the two groups on the first visit? Were the drop-outs sicker, did they smoke more, were they physiologically or chronologically older?

9. Finally, when all is said and done, can we really feel certain that anything we discover about aging in man will really be applicable to the rat?

In the time remaining, I want to discuss one aspect of the experimental design of aging studies in man. If the hypotheses being tested require the longitudinal approach, then certain strategic design questions must be answered: How long should the study continue? How often should the subjects be tested? In a cross-sectional study, we might get an idea in February, work out the methodology in March,

get approval of the local Human Experimentation Committee
in April, recruit the subjects in May, study them in June,
submit the paper in July, have it published in November
and be famous by Christmas. What would your mathematical
intuition tell you about how long each of these steps might
take for a longitudinal rather than for a cross-sectional
study? Even neglecting the more complex experimental
design and the increased difficulties of getting approval
from funding sources and from Human Experimentation Commit-
tees, the rate-limiting step in the research is bound to be
that single month of June during which data were collected
in the cross-sectional study. Well, how long does one need
to study a group of individuals in order to define their
aging rates? Would you guess 3 years or 5 years or 10
years? And while these years are going by, just how often
should measurements be carried out? At the beginning,
middle, and end of the study? Every year?

We have recently given some quantitative consideration
to these questions. Two papers have recently been published by our statistical collaborator, Dr. James Schlesselman
(1973a, b). I will present here only a summary of the
theory and application of the techniques that he developed.

Consider first a variable which declines progressively
with age and which is measured with great accuracy and re-
producibility. Body height is an example of such a variable. In contrast, consider a variable such as basal
diastolic blood pressure (DBP) which increases progressively with age but which has a large variance in its measurement from day to day or even from moment to moment. Intui-
tively one can appreciate that the rate of decrease in body
height could be estimated with fewer measurements and over
a shorter period of time than could the rate of increase
of DBP.

This intuition does not, however, allow one to design
an efficient longitudinal study in quantitative terms.
Here we turn to Dr. Schlesselman's papers (1973a, b). The
standard error in estimating a slope as obtained in longitudinal studies of aging varies inversely as D (the duration of the study) and inversely as the <u>square root</u> of P
(the number of tests performed). Thus, in a 5-year study
with annual examinations (6 exams in 5 years), the error
in estimating the slope can be halved by carrying out 6
exams in 10 years or, if the study must be completed in 5
years, by carrying out 20 tests in that period!

But, back to the decision-making process: How can the scientist, in advance, plan the D and the P of a longitudinal study? The important formula is derived by Schlesselman as:

[1] $\omega = CV\ (\hat{b})/\sigma.$

A few definitions are needed:

$\hat{b}$ = the slope

$SE(\hat{b})$ = standard error of the slope

σ = standard error of the estimate of the slope

[2] CV = coefficient of variation = $SE(\hat{b})/\hat{b}.$

ω, as defined mathematically above and as used in Tables I-III of Schlesselman (1973b).

Several points can be made: $\hat{b}$ and σ are biological characteristics and are therefore fixed by nature not by the experimenter. But, $SE(\hat{b})$ is under the investigator's control, since he can, by increasing D or P or both, decrease the value of $SE(\hat{b})$ and thereby increase the accuracy of his <u>estimate</u> of $\hat{b}$.

Referring back to Formula [1], it is obvious that $\hat{b}$ and σ must be known and a suitable CV decided upon before ω can be calculated. But $\hat{b}$ and σ cannot be known unless a longitudinal study has previously been done! Lacking these data, the designer will have to use educated guesses for these values. Thus, he could use data from cross-sectional studies as a starting point.

In our own study, we have just begun to generate ω's for a number of physiological variables and these will be reported in detail elsewhere. I can summarize these preliminary data with this uncomfortable conclusion: With the usual examination schedule adopted by most longitudinal studies of human aging (once, yearly or bi-yearly), most physiological variables will require some 15 to 20 years of testing in order to define rates of aging in a majority of subjects with acceptable accuracy.

There are, however, some rays of optimism to consider as the years of waiting go by. There is a remarkable "fall-out" in the performance of a longitudinal study of aging. Cross-sectional data are constantly being produced, and secular trends in the population are being followed. Furthermore, a panel of longitudinal participants provides a continuing source of potential volunteers for a wide variety of what might be called one-shot studies of aging. We are, for example, studying the mechanisms underlying the decreasing glucose tolerance with age, by means of series of tests which are complex and difficult to perform. We do not intend to administer these tests to all of our subjects and probably will not be repeating them slavishly through the years. But we have been able to select participants with just those characteristics which would provide us with the most information per study.

There is an important implication in our analyses of longitudinal data. Since we believe it will require some 15 to 20 years to define aging rates well, the difficulty will be compounded when we ask whether a potential therapeutic or prophylactic regimen has altered the rate of aging. This question implies that two rates have been accurately defined, a "before" and an "after" rate. Entering into clinical trials of anti-aging drugs in man should be undertaken when other evidence of effectiveness (and, of course, safety) is indeed very strong.

ACKNOWLEDGEMENT

Discussions over the years with the senior scientists of the Baltimore Longitudinal Study, Drs. Nathan W. Shock and Jordan D. Tobin and Mr. Arthur H. Norris, as well as with many younger scientists at the Gerontology Research Center have been essential to the development of the ideas expressed in this paper. They should, however, not be held responsible for the gaucheries that crept into the presentation.

REFERENCES

Schlesselman, J. J. (1973a). J. Chronic Diseases 25, 553.
Schlesselman, J. J. (1973b). J. Chronic Diseases 26, 561.

THEORETICAL AND PRACTICAL ASPECTS OF CHEMOTHERAPEUTIC TECHNIQUES IN THE RETARDATION OF THE AGING PROCESS

Ana Aslan, M.D., D.Sc.

The Bucharest Institute of Geriatrics
Bucharest, Romania

The chemotherapeutic techniques for the retardation of the aging process mentioned in the title refers primarily to procaine therapy. Between the years 1945 and 1951, the commercially available procaine hydrochloride solution was used (Aslan and Rosenzweig, 1946), after which Gerovital H_3 was employed. The latter preparation is a procaine solution with its pharmacologic action modified by a formulation to be described later in this presentation. When procaine therapy was originally tried 30 years ago, it was without any particular reference to the aging process. Rather, it was undertaken as a result of certain observations made during the treatment of patients with peripheral vascular disorders (Leriche and LaFontaine, 1953) or suffering from angina pectoris (Ameuille, 1949) and asthma (Dos Ghali et al., 1943). The favorable results obtained in these patients were considered to be due to the vasodilating, anesthetic and analgesic property of procaine.

It was at this time that we decided to extend this treatment to selected patients with joint disease and, in 1949, I initiated a program of injecting procaine HCl intra-arterially in patients with certain forms of arthritis and arthrosis. The results were published with Vrabiescu in 1950. Usually the treatment consisted of injections into the femoral and subclavian arteries of the patients. While treating elderly patients with the intra-arterial approach, I observed generalized effects beyond those referable solely to the joints. Thus, improvement in the texture of skin, improved recall, increased psychomotor activity and muscle strength were noted. These findings led us into a systematic study of the use of procaine in the treatment of the aging process.

In May, 1951, the Bucharest Institute of Geriatrics was founded for the prime purpose of studying possible methods for the prevention and treatment of pathological signs of advancing age. Its research approach derived from Parhon's (1955) concept that the process of aging could be influenced, not only through hygienic measures, but also by developing substances which acted at the level of cellular metabolism, particularly those enhancing anabolic activity.

Initial long-term studies using chemotherapeutic agents were tested in the three groups of 30-40 elderly patients selected according to their clinical, physiological and biochemical state. They had already received a variety of exploratory treatments including splenic extracts, pineal gland, thyroid, procaine, vitamin E, and vitamin B complex. Out of these three selected groups, one group was put on procaine, the second on vitamin E, and the third on pineal gland extract (later this group became a control group), all being administered intramuscularly three times a week for a total of 12 injections over a four-week period. Then, after a 10-day drug-free interval, the series of injections were resumed. Eight series of injections were given during the first year, and the program was continued during subsequent years.

It didn't take too long to notice marked changes in the procaine group, in which hair repigmentation was noticed and reported, an effect of procaine which was, until then, unknown (Parhon and Aslan, 1953). Later, Parhon et al. (1955) published their "Results of Psychological Tests", reporting also an improvement in memory and attention by this procaine treatment. A large series of criteria were then developed to measure these changes objectively. Psychological test batteries, studies of conditioned reflexes, and tests of psychological reactivity were devised (David and Enachescu, 1965). By means of plethysmographic and oscillometric investigations, the vascular reactivity to various physical stimuli were measured (Aslan and Vrabiescu, 1955). Muscle strength and blood velocity measures were taken. Biochemical analyses to examine protein, lipid and glucose metabolism, as well as routine blood chemistries and blood counts were used. In addition, life expectancy, morbidity and mortality tables were employed to analyze how the three groups compared with each other and with the general population.

146

For the three experimental groups, the average age was: procaine, 72 years; vitamin E, 75 years; and controls, 73 years (Aslan, 1966). The patients in the study lived under similar environmental conditions, in the home section of the Geriatric Institute of Bucharest, and received the same food and care as the other patients not involved in the experimental procedure.

We would like to point out that, in 1952, we did not use the double-blind study model. Rather, we designed a longitudinal study with each patient serving as his own control. We focused our attention on all symptoms of aging with special attention to depression, memory impairment, degenerative arthritis and the various manifestations of arteriosclerosis (Aslan, 1957).

After the first two years of treatment, the results obtained in the three groups were analyzed and compared. Positive results were obtained in the procaine and less in the vitamin E groups. Long-term treatment was then continued for 13 additional years, and the mortality recorded for the entire 15-year period. The mortality was 5% for the procaine group, 10% for the vitamin E group, and 15% for the control group.

GEROVITAL H_3 vs. PROCAINE HC1

As mentioned before, in 1951, we discontinued the use of commercial procaine HC1, at which time Gerovital H_3 was developed.

There are differences in composition and pharmacological action between Gerovital H_3 and procaine. The molecular structure of procaine consists of an aromatic ring connected through an intermediate chain with an amino group, the linkage being by means of an ester linkage in the intermediate chain (Ellis and Littlejohn, 1974). Hazard (1949) had shown that commercially-available procaine preparations are not stable for more than a six-month period, at most. Thus, our efforts were concentrated on finding a procaine solution with a greater shelf as well as an *in vivo* half-life, i.e., after introduction to the animal or human body, than the then existing commercial preparations. In other words, to prolong as much as possible the half-life of the whole molecule of procaine, taking into consideration that the metabolic splinters, the para-aminobenzoic acid (PABA) and diethylaminoethanol (DEAE), while still active, are less so than the whole procaine molecule. The results of our research were expressed in the form of a new product, with a different formula, Gerovital H3. In this formula, the procaine HCl pharmacological action is modified through the addition of benzoic acid and potassium metabisulfate which also serve as antioxidant and preservative agents. The pH of Gerovital H_3 was 3.3.

The procaine molecule, after introduction into the human body, is known to be rapidly hydrolized by cholinesterase (or pseudo-cholinesterase, or procainesterase) into two metabolic fractions, PABA and DEAE. In the case of Gerovital H_3, thin-layer chromatographic techniques have shown that intact molecules of procaine can be found in blood and urine of experimental animals six hours after the administration of the drug (Biometric Testing, Inc., Englewood Cliffs, New Jersey, Dec. 1973 Report). There are two possible explanations for this important difference in procaine metabolism:

1. Ballard, et al. (1971) have demonstrated that procaine HCl injections differ significantly in their metabolic fate according to the pH of the solution. At pH 7.0, the procaine penetrates "en masse" into the blood stream. At pH 3.3, the procaine is released slowly into the blood stream, thus, the acidity of the solution apparently acts as a sustained release mechanism for procaine. It should be mentioned that this finding was reported 15 years after Gerovital H3, with a pH of 3.3, was first introduced. One year later, Dettburn, et al. (1972) reported that the pH of a procaine solution is critical as far as its penetration into body fluids is concerned, diminishing as the pH grows more acid.

2. A theory advanced by Jordan Cohen (1972) postulates that the benzoic acid forms a loose complex with the procaine molecule which is similar to the type of molecular complex formed between caffeine and procaine (Lachman et al., 1956). The benzoic acid moiety does seem to attach itself loosely to the intermediate chain of procaine, the weak point in the procaine molecule, thus protecting it from cholinesterase activity. Some support for this theory is furnished by thin-layer chromatography in which the

procaine band is accompanied closely by a benzoic or para-benzoic acid band (Biometrics, 1972).

Also of importance is the presence of the potassium ions in the Gerovital H_3, which potentiates the action of procaine on the nervous system and at the muscular level (Teitel et al., 1960).

Clinical support for the difference between Gerovital H_3 and procaine has been reported by a number of research-ers. First, the pharmacology and the clinical results obtained by using Gerovital H_3 and procaine are not the same as for commercial procaine (Gordon et al., 1963; Abrams and Gordon, 1964). Double-blind studies by Gordon and colleagues in 1965, in which patients were used and in which Gerovital H_3 was compared to procaine, revealed statistically significant differences in favor of Gerovital H_3 as compared to procaine. Investigations performed in collaboration with Parhon (1955) have consistently found significant differences between Gerovital H_3 and procaine in the induction of vascular conditional and unconditional reflexes in elderly patients. These results were confirmed in humans by Tsobkallo and Kucherenko (1961), and in dogs and rabbits, using salivary reflexes.

PABA and DEAE

Although we have concentrated our attention to this point only on the pharmacological and biological aspects of the intact procaine molecule, the metabolic splinter products, PABA and DEAE, also deserve notice. While pro-caine is a chemical compound, PABA and DEAE are actual biological components normally found in the human organism where they perform vital metabolic functions. For example, PABA is called "vitamin factor H_1", by Kuhn (1948). Bran-bury and Jordan (1961) have shown that both PABA and pro-caine act at the level of cell membrane metabolism.

We have investigated the action of Gerovital H_3 and PABA on infusorian protozoa. Higher levels of cell pro-liferation were found with Gerovital H_3 than with PABA. At the same time, the appearance of a yellow pigment in the cell culture was noted (Aslan, 1958). This pigment was also found by Mayer (1944) in researches on mycobacter-ium tuberculosis.

With Leonida and Coniver (1958), I have studied the vitamin-like action of procaine and PABA on Staphylococcus aureus and Entamoeba coli, both cultured in a 2% glucose nutrient solution. PABA was shown to have a vitamin-like action at concentrations of 0.001%, whereas procaine had a similar effect at concentrations of 0.00124%.

A series of further investigations then proposed the hypothesis that procaine, through PABA, could stimulate intestinal microflora to produce certain biogenic factors such as folic acid, vitamin K and thiamine. Together with Nicholae and Jantea (1963), I observed that old patients treated with Gerovital H$_3$ showed an increase in the intestinal content of an aerobic lactobacillus as compared to controls. This lactobacillus inhibits the growth of proteolytic microorganisms. Likewise, after administration of Gerovital H$_3$, we observed an increase in the growth of colibacilli whose number are generally reduced in patients over 70. In the Gerovital H$_3$-treated geriatric patients, higher folic acid levels were found as compared to the control group (Aslan et al., 1969). This increase was attributed to the stimulation of intestinal microbial flora by the PABA. As is well known, the PABA resulting from procaine hydrolysis constitutes a source of supply available for the synthesis of folic acid. Also, DEAE apparently participates in the synthesis of choline and acetylcholine (Groth et al., 1950).

CLINICAL STUDIES IN THE UNITED STATES

Bucci and Saunders (1960), in applying our method, pointed out the favorable effect of this treatment in elderly schizophrenic patients. They reported the disappearance of hallucinations, renewed contact with the environment and a recovery of intellectual activity in such patients. These authors, quoting Philpot (1940), considered the drug's action to be related to the inhibition of monoamine oxidase (MAO) by Gerovital H$_3$. Bucci (1973) again confirmed the action of procaine as a MAO inhibitor, in association with chlorpromazine in complete recoveries of 16 out of 20 patients suffering from schizophrenia. Long (1964) likewise investigated the effects of procaine on orientation, memory, attention and body weight of old people. He applied our method for one year, carrying out a double-blind trial of 60 elderly subjects

150

suffering from disorders of orientation. An evaluation
system especially designed to measure orientation, memory
and attention revealed that the treated group performed
better than the control group. The ability to memorize
was improved in the treated group and worsened in the control group. Body weight also increased in the treated
and decreased in the control group.

Kral et al. (1962) treated geriatric patients with
procaine in accordance with our methods. He reported
favorable, but transitory results in the relief of depressed states of the aging patient.

Cohen and Ditman, in 1973, performed an open study
with Gerovital H_3 in old, depressed patients (Cohen and
Ditman, 1974). They reported prompt and dramatic (but
mainly subjective) improvement of depression in 35 out of
45 patients. Those who improved felt a greater sense of
well-being and relaxation, slept better, mentioned relief
from depression and less discomfort from chronic inflamma-
tory or degenerative disorders. One unexpected result was
that those with elevated cholesterol levels (mean 339.3)
before treatment had a decrease after a single series of
Gerovital H_3 to a mean of 288.5. It is of interest to note
that Parhon and Aslan reported, in 1954, the decrease in
cholesterol levels in blood of patients treated with procaine. Gershon et al. (1974), in single-blind studies
conducted in 1973, using Gerovital H_3 in depressed, aged
patients, reported that significant results were obtained
in the third week of treatment, when Gerovital H_3 was administered in a regimen of two vials of 10 ml Gerovital H_3
or 200 mg procaine HCl, three times a week. We have to
mention that, with few exceptions (as it is in the treatment of scleroderma), our method involves a one-month
series of 12 injections(each of one 5 ml dose)of Gerovital
H_3. As you may know, at the present time, double-blind
studies of Gerovital H_3 are being carried out on humans
in several universities and research centers in the United
States.

GEROVITAL H_3, A MONOAMINE OXIDASE INHIBITOR

For many years beneficial effects were claimed for
Gerovital H_3 in a variety of unrelated disorders associated
with the aging process such as hypertension, arthritis,
angina pectoris, depression, and certain other conditions.
That such a wide range of claims should be greeted with

151

skepticism by some medical authorities is understandable.
While I understood this attitude very well, I and other
clinicians meanwhile pursued our trials of the drug with
good results and continued to keep our medical colleagues
informed of our work. However, it is of interest to note
that, in 1960, Bucci and Saunders found that prolonged
treatment with procaine was clinically effective in re-
lieving depression and ameliorating psychotic symptoms
associated with schizophrenia. They were the first to
speculate that these results were due to a possible inhibitory effect of procaine on the monoamine oxidase system.
In 1970, Lifshitz and Kline (in "Psychopharmacology in
Geriatrics") also proposed that procaine might be a monoamine oxidase inhibitor (MAOI). No further work was done on
this matter until 1972 when MacFarlane and Hrachovec, both
at the School of Pharmacy at U. S. C., each reported that
Gerovital H_3 was, indeed, a MAO inhibitor. They reported
that the rate of inhibition for Gerovital H_3, compared with
that of commercially-available procaine, was statistically,
significantly higher.

Work performed by Yau (1973) and others has confirmed
the inhibitory action of Gerovital H_3 on MAO. Thus, one
aspect of the 20-year controversy surrounding Gerovital H_3
was clarified, because monoamine oxidase inhibitors in
general have been reported to be beneficial for the very
same conditions for which we had previously claimed im-
provements by Gerovital H_3, namely depression, hypertension, arthritis, and angina pectoris.

The next question that arose was why other MAO inhibitors are accompanied by severely adverse, sometimes fatal
side effects, whereas Gerovital H_3 has almost no side
effects at all. Allergic reactions to Gerovital H_3 have
occurred in only about 1 out of 6,000 cases. The work by
MacFarlane (1973a, b) and his group during the past two
years, and of Yau (1973), has brought forth significant, new
relevant data. In a paper presented at the 26th Annual
Meeting of the Gerontological Society in Miami, in November,
1973, MacFarlane showed that the known MAO inhibitors
(Pargyline, for example) are strong, irreversible MAO
inhibitors and produce a mixed non-competitive-competitive
inhibition of the enzyme. Gerovital H_3, on the other
hand, is a weak, reversible and fully competitive MAO inhibitor. MacFarlane further stated that, while patients
receiving the traditional irreversible MAO inhibitors may

experience severe, sometimes fatal side effects, such as paroxysmal hypertension culminating in intracranial hemor- rhage, after eating tyramine-containing foods such as certain cheeses or wines, these reactions have never been reported in patients receiving Gerovital H_3. Food restric- tions are quite unnecessary in connection with Gerovital H_3 therapy. Further, in a communication presented at this Symposium on the "Theoretical Aspects of Aging", held in Miami on February 7-8, 1974, Yau showed that Gerovital H_3 is a selective inhibitor of MAO, not only as regards vari- ous substrates of the MAO, but for a number of different organs as well.

MONOAMINE OXIDASE AND AGING

A recent report by Robinson et al. (1972) in Lancet has relevance to the question of MAO inhibitors and the disorders of aging. This paper represented the research results from five collaborating groups of investigators in England and the United States. Its title is: "Aging, Monoamines and Monoamine Oxidase Levels." The principal point of the article is that increased levels of activity of the enzyme, monoamine oxidase, are related not only to the phenomenon of depression, but likewise to the aging process itself. It was clearly shown that, after the age of 45-50, activity levels of monoamine oxidase are dramati- cally elevated with a reciprocal decline in norepinephrine levels.

MacFarlane (1973a) proposed the idea that, perhaps, the clinical results of Gerovital H_3 in aged patients are due to a tendency to bring MAO and norepinephrine levels back toward normal.

Long before Robinson's (1972) study was published, I recommended preventive treatment with Gerovital H_3, start- ing at age 45. It is precisely at this age that the Robinson et al. (1972) study found that MAO levels in- crease, while those of norepinephrine decline in patients receiving Gerovital H_3. As the weeks and months pass, more research work in the experimental and clinical fields with Gerovital H_3 is being initiated in the United States. As they appear, the results, I am happy to say, continue to confirm the experimental and clinical work done by me over the past two decades.

With me here today at this Symposium are three young

153

colleagues whose research findings with Gerovital H_3 on the cell membrane, on tissue cultures and on monoamine oxidase are remarkable. To me, their results are a source of great personal satisfaction that more than make up for the misunderstandings and, perhaps, doubts of the past. I am firmly convinced that, as work with Gerovital H_3 continues in the United States, more issues as to its pharmacological importance will be clarified to the satisfaction of all of us who are interested in the problems of aging.

REFERENCES

Abrams, A. and Gordon, P. (1964). Excerpta Med. XX, 4, 163.

Ameuille, A. (1949). Méd. Jour 5, 198.

Aslan, A. (1957). Therapiewoche 1, 10.

Aslan, A. (1958). Arzneimittel-Forsch. 8, 11.

Aslan, A. (1966). Inter. Congr. Gerontol. (Vienna) Austria, 764, 268.

Aslan, A., Cirje, M. and Nicolae, M. (1969). Prophylaxe 8, 25.

Aslan, A., Leonida, C. and Coniver, M. (1958). Unpublished data.

Aslan, A., Nicolae, D., Jantea, F. and Dumitrescu, Z. (1963). Giorn. Gerontol. XIII, 772.

Aslan, A. and Rosenzweig, S. (1946). Bull. Rom. Acad. Med. 7, 891.

Aslan, A. and Vrabiescu, A. (1950). Bull. Rom. Acad. Sci. 2, 891.

Aslan, A. and Vrabiescu, A. (1955). Endocrine Res. 6, 215.

Ballard, B. E., Menczel, E. and Yacobi, A. (1971). APhA Acad. Pharm. Sci. Sess. 118th Annual Meeting of the Am. Pharm. Assoc., San Francisco, Calif., March 27 - April 2, Vol. I.

Branbury, M. and Jordan, J. (1961). In "Ferments, Hormones and Vitamins" (G. Thieme, ed.), Leipzig, Germany.

Bucci, L. (1973). Diseases Nervous System 7, 389.

Bucci, L. and Saunders, J. C. (1960). J. Neuropsychiat. 5, 276.

Cohen, J. (1972). Unpublished data.

Cohen, S. and Ditman, K. (1974). Psychosomatics 1, 15.

David, D. and Enachescu, C. (1965). Therapiewoche 3, 149.

Dettburn, W. D., Heilinson, E., Hoskin, F. C. C. and Kitz, R. (1972). Nemopharm. 11, 727.

Dos Ghali, J., Bourdain, J. S. and Guillot, C. (1941).
Bull. Soc. Méd. Hôp. Paris, p. 741.
Ellis, P. P. and Littlejohn, K. (1974). Am. J. Ophthalmol.
77, 71.
Gershon, S., Sakalis, G. and Shopsin, B. (1974). Current
Therap. Res. 16, 59.
Gordon, P., Fudema, J. and Abrams, A. (1963). The Gerontol-
ogist, II.
Gordon, P., Fudema, J., Snider, G. L., Abrams, A., Tobin,
S. S. and Kraus, J. D. (1965). J. Gerontol. 20, 144.
Groth, D. F., Bain, J. A. and Pfeiffer, C. C. (1950). J.
Pharmacol. Exp. Therap. 122, 20 A.
Hazard, M. (1949). Méd. Jour 5, 190.
Hrachovec. J. P. (1972). The Physiologist 3, 12.
Kuhn, B. (1948). In "Ferments, Hormones and Vitamins" (G.
Thieme, ed.), p. 754, 1617, Leipzig, Germany.
Kral. V. A., Cahn, C. and Deutsch, M. (1962). Can. Med.
Assoc. J. 87, 1109.
Lachman, L., Ravin, L. J. and Higuchi, T. (1956). J. Am.
Pharm. Assoc. XLV, 290.
Leriche, R. and LaFontaine, R. (1953). Presse Med. 17, 327.
Lifshitz, G. and Kline, N. S. (1970). In "Principles of
Psychopharmacology" (W. G. Clark and J. del Guidice,
eds.), pp. 704-705, Academic Press, New York.
Long, F. R. (1964). J. Neuropsychiat. 5, 186.
MacFarlane, M. D. (1972). The Lancet 7772, 337.
MacFarlane, M. D. (1973a). J. Am. Geriat. Soc. 21, 414.
MacFarlane, M. D. (1973b). 26th Annual Meeting Gerontol.
Soc., Miami, Florida, November, 1973.
Mayer, R. L. (1958). J. Bacteriol. 1, 93.
Parhon, C. I. (1955). "Biologia Virstelor (The Biology of
the Ages-Clinical and Experimental Researches)."
Romanian Academy, Bucharest.
Parhon, C. I. and Aslan, A. (1954). Bull. Rom. Acad. Sci.
4, 557.
Parhon, C. I., Aslan, A. and Vrabiescu, A. (1955). Bull.
Rom. Acad. Sci. 5, 417.
Philpot, F. J. (1940). J. Physiol. 97, 301.
Robinson, D. S., Davis, J. M., Nies, A., Colburn, R. W.,
Davis, J. N., Bourne, H. R., Bunney, W. E., Shaw, D. M.
and Coppen, A. J. (1972). The Lancet 7745, 290.
Teitel, A., Marcu, C. and Popa, A. (1960). Natl. Conf.
Physiol., Rom. Acad. Sci., Bucharest, p. 156.

Tsobkallo, G. I. and Kucherenko, T. M. (1961). Inter. Conf.
    Pharmacol., Stockholm, August 22-25, 1961.
Yau, T. M. (1973). 26th Annual Meeting Gerontol. Soc.,
    Miami, Florida, November 1973.

GEROVITAL H$_3$, MONOAMINE OXIDASES,
AND BRAIN MONOAMINES

Tom M. Yau, Ph.D.

Ohio Mental Health and
Mental Retardation Research Center
Cleveland, Ohio 44109

Advancing age is frequently accompanied by disorders
of mental function and mood (Roth, 1955; Silverman, 1968).
At present, most biochemical and psychopharmacological data
all tend to support the biogenic amine hypothesis of
affective disorders which states that mental depression may
be associated with a deficiency of catecholamines (Bunney
and Davis, 1965; Schildkraut, 1965) or indoleamines
(Coppen, 1967) at functionally important receptor sites in
the brain. Based on the observations that monoamine
oxidase (MAO) activity increases and norepinephrine level
decreases with age in the human hindbrain, Robinson and his
colleagues (1968) speculated that "this relationship of
age to enzyme might be a predisposing factor to depression
which accentuates changes in brain amines precipitated by
other events".

Aging can be defined as a normal biological process
accompanied by the gradual loss of adaptability both physiologically and behaviorally until the eventual death of
the organism. Although the vicious-cycle nature of these
two intrinsic factors and the undesirable consequences of
their complex interactions are inevitable, the process of
aging may be retarded, theoretically to a certain extent,
by pharmacological intervention. However, one should bear
in mind that the aged are a population at risk. Granted,
the assumption that psychiatric depression is one of the
most common manifestations that aggrevates the severity of
other symptoms related to aging, factors such as over-
medication, drug-drug interaction, tolerance to drug
toxicity and inherent side effects, ought to be evaluated
indiscriminately before any psychotropic agents are

157

prescribed to the aged (Learoyd, 1972). Undeniably, the
margin of error in this population is markedly reduced.

Among the different categories of antidepressants
available, the tricyclic compounds and the MAO inhibitors
have contributed significantly both in their demonstrated
clinical efficacy and in lending themselves as a tool for
the elucidation of basic mechanisms underlying depressive
illness and psychopharmacology (Klerman, 1972). In recent
years however, MAO inhibitors in comparison to tricyclic
compounds are in relative disuse. They frequently predis-
pose to interactive toxicity with other drugs, food ingre-
dients, and are inherently toxic (Goldberg, 1964). Nevertheless, the drug industry is still actively pursuing
better MAO inhibitors devoid of adverse side effects. The
reason for this is two-fold. First, there always remains
a segment of tricyclic-resistant depressed patients who
are specific MAO responders (Schiele, 1965; Pare et al.,
1962; Pare and Mack, 1971). Secondly, the existence of
multiple molecular forms of MAO with differential substrate
and inhibitor specificities have unveiled new possibilities
in the treatment of heterogeneous affective disorders. New
MAO inhibitors within the realm of synthetic feasibility
may be expected to inhibit particular forms of MAO and
thereby altering the level of specific brain monoamines.
It is evident that many rigid requirements would have to
be met in order for a new MAO inhibitor to be accepted by
the medical profession, especially in the treatment of depressive illness in the aged.

Gerovital H_3 (GH_3), with 2% procaine as its active
ingredient, has been used in the treatment of symptoms related to old age for more than 20 years (Aslan, 1956). The
ability of procaine to inhibit MAO has recently been advo-
cated as a possible rationale for its clinical efficacy
(Hrachovec, 1972; MacFarlane, 1973a). In contrast to the
properties of other classical MAO inhibitors, it was subsequently demonstrated that GH_3 is a weak, reversible and
competitive inhibitor of MAO (MacFarlane, 1973b). In our
laboratory, we have further pursued the nature of MAO inhibition exerted by GH_3 both in vivo and in vitro in inbred
BL57/10j mice.

The effects of GH_3 on the level of monoamines in the
mouse forebrain are presented in Table I. In contrast to
results with other MAO inhibitors (Spector et al., 1963;
Tozer et al., 1966), the increase in brain monoamines two

TABLE I

Effects of varying Gerovital H$_3$ dosage on maze index and
on the endogenous level of monoamines in mouse forebrain
two hours after injection. Each value given is an average
for six animals.

SALINE	GH$_3$(90mg/Kg)	GH$_3$(120mg/Kg)	GH$_3$(180mg/Kg)
MAZE INDEX			
267.4±22	193.2±25 (72%)*	176.0±55 (66%)	51.5±17 (19%)
NOREPINEPHRINE (µg/Gm)			
0.53±0.03	0.60±0.03 (113%)	0.60±0.03 (113%)	0.63±0.001 (119%)
DOPAMINE (µg/Gm)			
2.59±0.18	3.07±0.18 (119%)	3.04±0.24 (117%)	2.96±0.27 (114%)
SEROTONIN (µg/Gm)			
1.11±0.08	1.26±0.17 (114%)	1.37±0.11 (123%)	1.44±0.12 (130%)

*( )=Percent change of control

159

hours after intraperitoneal injection of GH3 is slight, but significant. With the possible exception of serotonin, no definite linear dose response is observed. The endogenous level of dopamine is actually slightly lower with higher GH3 dosage. In the same experiment, definite sedative effect of GH3 was also demonstrated. The maze index is inversely proportional to drug dosage.

In a separate experiment, the effect of chronic GH3 injection on the level of monoamines in mouse forebrain was studied. Either GH3 (60mg/Kg) or a saline control was administered intraperitoneally to three groups of six mice each, (5, 12, and 19 months of age) three times a week for four consecutive weeks. The animals were sacrificed 24 hours after the last injection. In view of the reversible and competitive nature of GH3 inhibition, and the results from Table I, it is not surprising that the effects are very minimal under these experimental conditions (Table II). A 10-20% increase in brain serotonin is observed. There is no change in the endogenous content of norepinephrine. Again, some interesting results were observed with dopamine. The decrease in dopamine level may be attributed to some delicate metabolic regulatory mechanism (Costa and Neff, 1966; Spector et al., 1967).

Multiple forms of monoamine oxidase may be isolated from mammalian tissues by various physiochemical methods (Youdim, 1973; Kim and D'Iorio, 1968). Selective inhibition exerted by MAO inhibitors (Hardegg and Heilbronn, 1961; Squires, 1972; Johnston, 1968; Hall et al., 1969), differential substrate specificity (Satake, 1955; Hope and Smith, 1960) and varying sensitivity to pH (Barbato and Abood, 1963) or heat inactivation (Youdim and Sourkes, 1965) represent other lines of evidence for the existence of multiple MAO in different species and in different tissues. Since the choice of substrate strongly influences the degree of inhibition of MAO by MAO inhibitors, we have studied the selective inhibition of GH3 and another two MAO inhibitors on the oxidative deamination of ^{14}C-labeled benzylamine, tyramine, tryptamine, dopamine and serotonin by mouse brain mitochondria. The results expressed as percent inhibition are summarized in figure 1. GH3 at 10^{-6}M is relatively insensitive to the oxidative deamination of benzylamine, but is quite active in inhibiting the oxidative deamination of brain serotonin at comparable concentrations. The pattern of inhibition is almost

TABLE II

Endogenous level of monoamines in mouse forebrain after chronic administration of Gerovital H_3 (60 mg/Kg, 3 times per week for four consecutive weeks). Animals were sacrificed 24 hours after the last injection. Each value is an average of six animals.

	SALINE			GH_3 60mg/Kg		
	5 M	12 M	19 M	5 M	12 M	19 M
NOREPINEPHRINE (μg/Gm)						
	0.51±0.03	0.49±0.03	0.50±0.03	0.49±0.03 (96%)*	0.50±0.04 (102%)	0.49±0.01 (98%)
DOPAMINE (μg/Gm)						
	2.65±0.12	2.65±0.22	2.98±0.43	2.29±0.22 (86%)	2.42±0.16 (91%)	2.25±0.17 (76%)
SEROTONIN (μg/Gm)						
	0.95±0.11	0.97±0.09	0.93±0.22	1.04±0.19 (109%)	1.14±0.13 (118%)	1.08±0.17 (116%)

*( )=Percent change of the corresponding control.

reversed with iproniazid, with comparatively little inhibition on dopamine and serotonin at 10^{-6} and $10^{-5}M$. Similar to iproniazid, the component of mouse brain MAO responsible for the deamination of benzylamine is most severely inhibited by isocarboxazid.

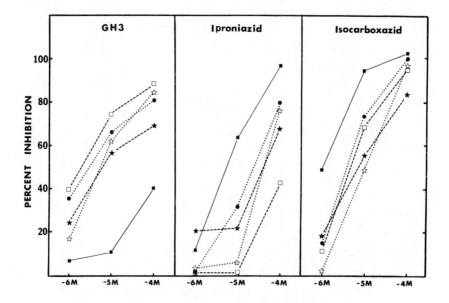

Fig. 1 Inhibition of mouse brain MAO by Gerovital H_3, Iproniazid, and Isocarboxazid. Substrates used were ^{14}C-labeled benzylamine ■——■ ; tyramine ●····●; tryptamine ☆····☆ ; dopamine ★----★ ; and serotonin □----□ .

The differential inhibition of GH_3 exerted on MAO of mouse brain, liver and heart is presented in figure 2. Apart from the overall evidence that MAO inhibition by GH_3 is most selective in the brain tissue, the relatively minimal inhibition of the deamination of tyramine or tryptamine in the liver is of great clinical significance. This may explain why patients treated with GH_3 are still permitted to consume tyramine-containing food (Sakalis et al., 1974). With the administration of other types of MAO inhibitors, abstinence from tyramine-containing food is mandatory (Blackwell, 1963; Robinson et al., 1968).

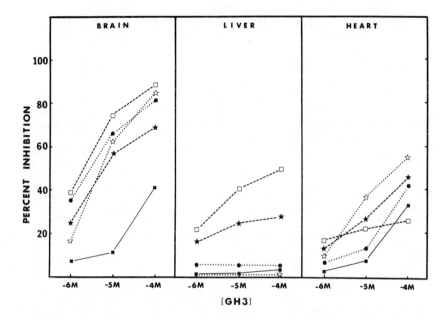

Fig. 2 Inhibition of mouse brain, liver and heart MAO by Gerovital H_3. Substrates used were ^{14}C-labeled benzylamine ■————■ ; tyramine ●••••● ; tryptamine ☆••••☆ ; dopamine ★----★ ; and serotonin □----□ .

Based on previous reports and additional results presented herein, the following conclusions can be made regarding the basic mechanisms of GH_3:

1) GH_3 is a weak, reversible and competitive inhibitor of MAO.

2) GH_3 may function as an antidepressant by gently modifying the level of brain monoamines.

3) Compared with a few classical MAO inhibitors, GH_3 is quite selective in inhibiting the oxidative deamination of certain important brain monoamines, especially serotonin.

163

4) Due to the minimal inhibition of GH$_3$ on the oxidative deamination of liver tyramine and tryptamine, the normal physiological function of liver MAO to inactivate excess amounts of ingested or endogenously synthesized toxic amines is not impaired, thereby eliminating the toxic "hypertensive crisis" so typical of other MAO inhibitors.

Through continuing research on GH$_3$ and similar reversible and selective MAO inhibitors, it is anticipated that successful dissociation of therapeutic efficacy from toxicity may finally be achieved.

REFERENCES

Aslan, A. (1956). Therapiewoche 7, 14.

Barbato, L. M. and Abood, L. G. (1963). Biochim. Biophys. Acta 67, 531.

Blackwell, B. (1963). Lancet 2, 849.

Bunney, W. E., Jr. and Davis, J. M. (1965). Arch. Gen. Psychiat. 13, 483.

Coppen, A. (1967). Brit. J. Psychiat. 113, 1237.

Costa, E. and Neff, N. H. (1966). In "Biochemistry and Pharmacology of the Basal Ganglia" (E. Costa, L. J. Côte and M. D. Yahr, eds.), pp. 141-155, Raven Press, New York.

Goldberg, L. I. (1964). J. Am. Med. Assoc. 190, 456.

Hall, D. W. R., Logan, B. W. and Parsons, G. H. (1969). Biochem. Pharmacol. 18, 1447.

Hardegg, W. and Heilbronn, E. (1961). Biochim. Biophys. Acta 51, 553.

Hope, D. B. and Smith, A. D. (1960). Biochem. J. 74, 101.

Hrachovec, J. P. (1972). Fed. Proc. 31, 604.

Johnston, J. P. (1968). Biochem. Pharmacol. 17, 1285.

Kim, H. C. and D'Iorio, A. (1968). Can. J. Biochem. 46, 296.

Klerman, G. L. (1972). J. Psychiat. Res. 9, 253.

Learoyd, B. M. (1972). Med. J. Australia 1, 1131.

MacFarlane, M. D. (1973a). J. Am. Geriat. Soc. 21, 414.

MacFarlane, M. D. (1973b). 26th Annual Meeting Gerontol. Soc., Miami, Florida, Nov. 1973.

Pare, C. M. B. and Mack, J. W. (1971). J. Med. Genet. 8, 306.

Pare, C. M. B., Rees, L. and Sainsbury, M. J. (1962). Lancet 2, 1340.

Robinson, D. S., Lovenberg, W., Keiser, H. and Sjoerdsma,

A. (1968). Biochem. Pharmacol. 17, 109.
Roth, M. (1955). J. Mental Sci. 101, 281.
Sakalis, G., Oh, D., Gershon, G. and Shopsin, B. (1974).
    Current Therap. Res. 16, 59.
Satake, K. (1955). Sakinno Kosokazaku 4, 39.
Schiele, B. C. (1965). Minn. Med. 48, 355.
Schildkraut, J. J. (1965). Am. J. Psychiat. 122, 509.
Silverman, C. (1968). "The Epidemiology of Depression."
    Johns Hopkins Press, Baltimore.
Spector, S., Gordon, R., Sjoerdsma, A. and Udenfriend, S.
    (1967). Mol. Pharmacol. 3, 549.
Spector, S., Hirsch, C. W. and Brodie, B. B. (1963). J.
    Neuropharmacol. 2, 81.
Squires, R. F. (1972). In "Monoamine Oxidases - New Vistas"
    (E. Costa and M. Sandler, eds.), pp. 355-370, Raven
    Press, New York.
Tozer, T. N., Neff, N. H. and Brodie, B. B. (1966). J.
    Pharmacol. Exp. Therap. 153, 177.
Youdim, M. B. H. (1973). Brit. Med. Bull. 29, 120.
Youdim, M. B. H. and Sourkes, T. L. (1965). Can. J.
    Biochem. 43, 1305.

PROCAINE-HC1 GROWTH ENHANCING EFFECTS ON AGED
MOUSE EMBRYO FIBROBLASTS CULTURED IN VITRO

J. Earle Officer

Department of Pathology
University of Southern California
School of Medicine
Los Angeles, California

The advantage of cell cultures established from either
embryos or organs of normal animals to study certain aspects of the aging phenomena at the cellular level has been
described previously by Hayflick and Moorhead (1961), Hayflick (1965), as well as by Gelfant and Grove and by Hayflick in this symposium. Such preparations also offer the
opportunity to study the effects of different compounds on
various aging parameters. For example, Dr. Gelfant has
mentioned treating his cultures with hydrocortisone increased the cell generation number, the latter dependent on
the time of initiation of treatment. This has also been
reported by Cristofalo (1972) and Macieira-Coelho (1966).
Aslan et al. (1972) has reported prolonging the cellular
proliferation of both chick embryo and monkey cell cultures
by treating them with Gerovital H_3 (GH_3 - a buffered
procaine-HC1 solution supplied by Rom-Amer Pharmaceuticals,
Ltd., Beverly Hills, California). As described by Dr. Hayflick in this symposium, continued cultivation of a cell
strain causes a variety of changes in cell morphology and
fine structure, the most outstanding of which is cessation
of cell division. This event occurs in mouse cells after
only a few generations in vitro and can be likened to
senescence or phase III of human cell culture (Tuffery and
Baker, 1973).
We have used the mouse model system to assess the
effects of GH_3 on the different phases of aging. Mouse
embryo fibroblast cultures (MEF) were established from wild
mouse embryos in their 18th to 20th day of gestation. When
these MEF cultures were cultivated in a restrictive medium

167

containing "Minimum Essential Medium" (MEM) plus 2% fetal calf serum, their doubling rate was constant for approximately eight generations. They then increased in doubling time until the tenth to eleventh generation when they ceased to multiply. At this time, the cells became enlarged, sending out large filamentous processes or sometimes became vacuolated, ending in degeneration of the cell (Tuffery and Baker, 1973). When the same cells were cultured in an optimum medium composed of 10% fetal bovine serum and Eagle's MEM, the cells undergo the same number of generations, but after reaching the stationary phase (phase III) the cells, unlike those grown in the restrictive medium, spontaneously transform into a continuous cell line (Todaro and Green, 1963). In contrast to the normal cell strain, these cells now possess a capacity for indefinite multiplication. They also grow more rapidly and reach higher densities (Todaro and Green, 1963; Tuffery and Baker, 1973). When secondary MEF cell cultures were infected with the RNA C type virus derived from a wild mouse embryo (Gardner et al., 1973), they underwent the aging process much more rapidly than infected cells, becoming aged by the fifth generation when they ceased to multiply, and then transformed into a continuous cell line (Wallace and Officer, 1974).

Figure 1 shows the typical aging phenomenon of the MEF cultures. Normal cells multiply approximately at the same rate for the first eight to nine generations, then show an increase in the time required for doubling which was measured by the time to reach confluency. When young (1-6 passages) MEF cell cultures were treated with 0.5% GH3 (final concentration in medium or equivalent to 500 μg of procaine per ml) there was a slowing down of cell growth. This condition was reversed by the addition of 200 μg of calcium chloride per ml to the medium. When 0.5% GH3 was added to mature cell cultures (7-9 passages), there was an immediate decrease in the time necessary for doubling and the cells continued to divide for two to three generations beyond that of the controls. These are similar to results described by Dr. Gelfant when hydrocortisone was added to late-passage human cells. When the same concentration of GH3 was added to the cells after they had ceased to multiply, the cells did not regain the capacity to divide, but were maintained for a longer period of time than the untreated cells in both the restrictive medium and the optimum medium. GH_3 also prevented the cells from spontaneously transforming into a continuous cell line in the latter medium. GH_3, when added to RNA C type virus-infected cells, prevented the pathogenic effect manifested by the increased aging phenomenon and likewise prevented the transformation of the cells into a permanent cell line. When GH_3 (in concentrations varying from 0.5 to 1.0%) was added to the culture medium of either spontaneously or virus transformed cell lines, the cells became highly vacuolated within a few hours and tysed after 24-48 hours. The selective lysis is similar to that reported using another local anesthetic, Dibucaine HCl (Rifkin and Reich, 1971).

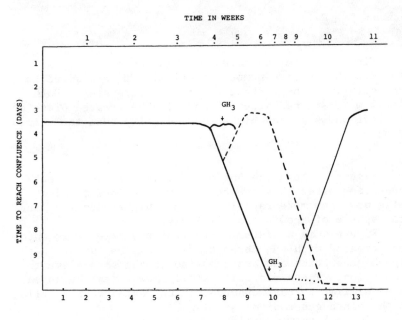

Fig. 1 Effect of Gerovital H_3 on the aging of mouse embryo fibroblasts <u>in vitro</u>.

Figure 2 shows sister cultures in the ninth generation. 0.5% GH_3 was added to the one on the right and both were stained after 48 hours. The treated culture showed a much higher density than the untreated culture.

Fig. 2   Sister cultures of wild mouse MEF cells
plated with the same number of cells. GH$_3$ was added to
the culture on the left at the time of transfer. Both
plates were stained after 48 hours. The treated plate on
the left shows a much higher cell density than the untreated one.

Figure 3 shows the untreated cells at the eleventh
generation after they spontaneously transformed. These
cells now grow more rapidly, reach a higher density, and
are capable of growing indefinitely.

Figure 4 is a sister culture of the same cells which
were treated with GH$_3$ three times weekly beginning in the
eighth generation and are now also in the same eleventh
generation. These old cells still show a healthy appearance, similar to that observed in untreated mature cells
in the ninth generation.

Figure 5 shows cells after cessation of growth (phase
III) in the tenth generation and then treated three times
weekly with GH$_3$. The cells were maintained in this condition for a period of several weeks and did not spontaneously transform like untreated cells.

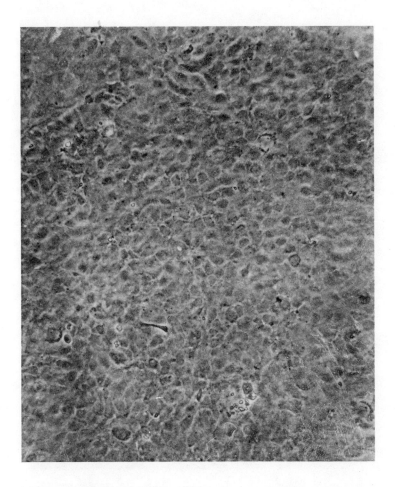

Fig. 3 Control MEF cell cultures in the eleventh generation which have spontaneously transformed into a continuous cell line.

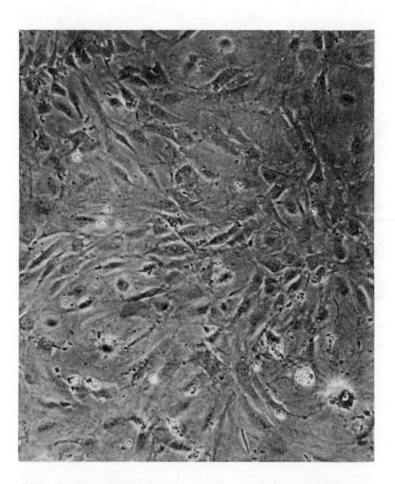

Fig. 4 MEF cell cultures were treated with GH_3 since the eighth generation and are now in the eleventh generation. These cells appear similar to untreated cells in the ninth generation.

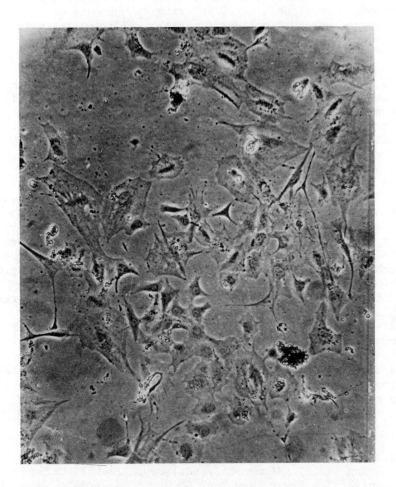

Fig. 5   MEF cell cultures that were treated with GH3
after they had reached the stationary phase of growth in
the tenth generation.   The cells were maintained in this
condition for a period of several weeks and did not spontaneously transform as did the untreated control cultures.

One of the consequences of cell aging is a decrease in membrane phospholipids with a concomitant increase in lecithin (Kristchevsky and Howard, 1966). As this decrease occurs, calcium apparently accumulates irreversibly in the cell membrane and thus is inaccessible for certain calcium dependent functions, e.g., activity of hormones on membrane-induced functions (Gusseck, 1972) and activation of adenyl cyclase for synthesis of cell regulating cyclic AMP (Rasmussen, 1970). The active compound of GH_3, procaine HCl, competes for and displaces membrane-bound calcium (Seeman, 1972), thus apparently releasing "irreversibly"-bound calcium into a reversible form, making it possible for the aged cell to continue to function in a normal manner. Thus the biological clock responsible for cell aging may indeed be the membrane of the cell, which is related to an accumulation of excess calcium which can be bound by hydrophilic chelators such as procaine, but not by hydrophobic chelators as EDTA.

These results correlate well with those of others who have reported nematodes treated with GH_3 delayed certain parameters characteristic of their aging process (Zuckerman, 1973). Furthermore, human erthrocyte membranes when treated with procaine remained elastic in contrast to the membranes of untreated erthrocytes which become very rigid when experimentally aged _in vitro_ (Baker, 1973). In addition, GH_3 has been shown to be an effective but reversible inhibitor of monoamine oxidase (MacFarlane, 1973; 1974), which is known to increase with age in tissues of humans and other animals (Robinson _et al._, 1971). These accumulative data lend strong support to previous claims made by Dr. Aslan (1962) concerning the possible ameliorative effects of Gerovital H_3, and offers possible rationals as to various modes of action on aging phenomena.

REFERENCES

Aslan, A. (1962). _In_ "Medical and Chemical Aspects of Aging" (H. T. Blumenthal, ed.), pp. 272-292, Columbia University Press, New York.

Aslan, A., Balan, L. and Ierema, G. (1972). _Fiziol. Norm. Pat._ 18, 81.

Baker, R. F. (1973). 26th Annual Meeting Gerontol. Soc., Miami, Florida, Nov. 1973.

Cristofalo, V. J. (1972). _Adv. Gerontol. Res._ 4, 45.

Gardner, M. B., Officer, J. E., Rongey, R. W., Charman, H. P., Hardy, J. W., Estes, J. D. and Huebner, R. J. (1973) Bibliotheca Haematol. (in press).

Gusseck, D. J. (1972). Adv. Gerontol. Res. 4, 105.

Hayflick, L. (1965). Exp. Cell Res. 37, 614.

Hayflick, L. and Moorhead, P. H. (1961). Exp. Cell Res. 25, 585.

Kristchevsky, D. and Howard, B. V. (1966). Ann. Med. Exp. Biol. Fenn. 44, 343.

MacFarlane, M. D. (1973). J. Am. Geriat. Soc. 21, 414.

MacFarlane, M. D. (1974). Fed. Proc. (in press).

Macieira-Coelho, A. (1966). Experientia 22, 390.

Rasmussen, H. (1970). Science 170, 404.

Rifkin, D. B. and Reich, E. (1971). Virology 45, 1971.

Robinson, D. S., Davis, J. N. and Neis, A. (1971). Arch. Gen. Psychiat. 24, 536.

Seeman, P. (1972). Pharm. Rev. 24, 583.

Todaro, G. J. and Green, H. (1963). J. Cell Biol. 17, 299.

Tuffery, A. A. and Baker, R. S. U. (1973). Exp. Cell Res. 76, 186.

Wallace, D. W. and Officer, J. E. (1974). Unpublished results.

Zuckerman, B. M. (1973). 26th Annual Meeting Gerontol. Soc. Miami, Florida, Nov. 1973.

THE EFFECTS OF PROCAINE ON AGING AND
DEVELOPMENT OF A NEMATODE

Bert M. Zuckerman[*]

Laboratory of Experimental Biology
University of Massachusetts
East Wareham, Massachusetts 02538

The free-living nematode, Caenorhabditis briggsae, is
being used in our laboratory to study the complex events
associated with biological aging. Our approach to this
problem involved first the defining of parameters characterizing senescence in this animal, and then evaluating the
effects on these aging signs of a drug reported to have a
modifying effect on some aspects of the aging processes.
Reference in this report to this preparation, Gerovital H$_3$
(2% procaine hydrochloride, 0.16% benzoic acid, 0.14%
potassium metabisulfite, buffered to pH 3.3 from Rom-Amer
Pharmaceuticals Ltd., Beverly Hills, California) is by its
active ingredient, "Procaine".

THE NEMATODE MODEL

The nematode possesses unique attributes for the study
of aging as a biological model. These include:

1. Ease of maintenance. C. briggsae can be maintained
in axenic culture utilizing standardized laboratory procedures (Sayre et al.,1963); complications introduced through
interactions with other organisms are therefore eliminated.

2. Small size. At maturity C. briggsae is about 1 mm
in length and 30 μ in width; thus large numbers can be
grown and maintained easily.

3. Constant cell number. With the exception of the
gonad, no new cells are formed after "hatch". Therefore,

---

*The work reported here was accomplished jointly with
Jessica M. Castillo and Marian J. Kisiel of the University
of Massachusetts Laboratory of Experimental Biology.

cellular aging throughout the life span can be followed in most tissues.

4. Differentiated cell systems of relatively simple morphology. C. briggsae contains nervous, muscle, excretory, digestive and reproductive systems, which, in total, comprise about 1,000 cells. Thus each system is composed of relatively few cells. Consequently, the elucidation of certain age-related changes should be far less difficult than comparable studies involving higher metazoa.

5. Short life span. C. briggsae matures in 4.5 days, stops reproducing at 14 days of age, and, on the average, dies in 28 days. Thus chronological aging occurs within relatively short time periods.

6. Shows signs of senescence. Moreover, at least some of the characteristics of aging in C. briggsae are similar to those of higher organisms, including man.

7. Availability of information. There have been numerous studies on the biochemistry of free-living nematodes (Krusberg, 1971) which provide a useful basis for the investigation of the physiology of aging.

AGING PARAMETERS

Recent investigations have defined a number of parameters characterizing senescence in C. briggsae. The most important of these are:

1. Age-related increases in specific gravity (Zuckerman et al., 1972) and in osmotic fragility (Zuckerman et al., 1971). A possible similarity of these changes to those of higher metazoa is indicated by the fact that increases in specific gravity and osmotic fragility with age also occur in human red blood cells (Danon and Marikovsky, 1964).

2. A progressive accumulation during aging of lipofuscin granules, commonly called age pigment (Buecher and Hansen, 1973; Epstein et al.,1972). Age pigment derives primarily from the peroxidation of lipids and its formation in certain tissues is also characteristic of aging in mammals (Kohn, 1971).

3. The accumulation with age of electron-dense materials within the cuticle median layer (Zuckerman et al.,

1973) and the pseudocoelom (Kisiel et al., in press). The nature of these materials is not known, but their location and appearance suggest the possibility that these masses are insoluble aggregates of cross-linked molecules. Bjorksten (1971) postulates that an increase in the number of crosslinkages with age is characteristic of aging in all animals.

4. A reduction in the net negative surface charge of the outer cuticular membrane of C. briggsae with age (Himmelhoch, Kisiel, Castillo and Zuckerman, unpublished data). A similar reduction in negative surface charges occurs during aging of rabbit and human erythrocytes (Danon et al., 1972).

Inactive enzyme molecules were shown to increase with age in another free-living nematode, Turbatrix aceti (Gershon and Gershon, 1970; Zeelon et al.,1973); however the design of these experiments necessitated use of a DNA synthesis inhibitor to attain age synchrony. Later studies showed that nematodes so treated were abnormal in many respects (Kisiel et al., 1972; Kisiel et al., in press), thus casting doubt on the validity of concluding from the nematode experiments alone that enzymatic aging has been demonstrated.

The elaboration of a broad spectrum of biological markers characterizing aging in C. briggsae was a preliminary requisite to a more detailed examination of aging in this organism. The parallel between several paths of deteriorative change in the nematode and in higher animals lends support to the belief that the study of C. briggsae will yield information important to the understanding of biological aging. In addition, the preceding studies have provided a frame-work within which chemicals which have been reported as affecting the aging processes can be examined.

THE EFFECTS OF PROCAINE ON DEVELOPMENT
AND AGING PARAMETERS

Under our culture conditions, C. briggsae normally starts reproducing 4.5 days after hatching and stops reproducing 9-10 days later. Dosages below 5 mg Procaine/ml medium (since all dosages were calculated as the amount of Procaine/ml medium, hereafter only the amount of Procaine will be specified) had no effect on the parameters evaluated, while above 10 mg, reproduction was completely inhibited in most tests. For a dose range of from 5 to 10 mg there was a progressively increasing delay in the inception of reproduction (i.e., the day on which the first larvae were observed), so that at 10 mg nematodes started to reproduce at about the same time as when reproduction normally ceases in untreated nematodes (figure 1).

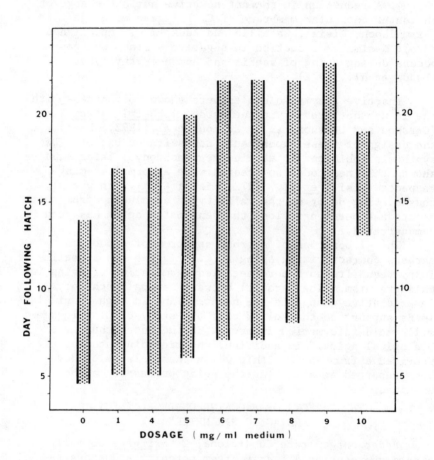

Fig. 1 Start and end of reproductive period of *Caenorhabditis briggsae* exposed to different levels of Procaine.

180

Unlike untreated cultures, there was great variation in the time that treated nematodes started to reproduce. Observations on individual nematodes exposed to 9 mg emphasized this differential delay in the onset of reproduction (Table I). This experiment also showed that the longer the delay in the start of reproduction, the shorter the reproductive period and the fewer the number of progeny.

TABLE I

Effects of 9 mg Procaine/ml medium on
reproduction of Caenorhabditis briggsae.[1]

Treatment	Start of reproduction after hatch (day)	Duration of reproduction (days)	Adults reproducing (%)	Number of offspring/ adult (Av.)
Untreated	4.5	10	100	104
Treated	8	10	18	46
Treated	9	8	18	39
Treated	10	9	20	30
Treated	11	6	15	14
Treated	12	5	2	13
Treated	16	1	2	3
Treated	17	1	2	1
Treated (complete inhibition)	-	-	23	0

[1]Figures represent averages from 60 individually cultured treated and 10 individually cultured untreated nematodes.

Comparative studies of untreated nematodes and those exposed to 9, 15, and 18 mg showed that the degree of inhibition of growth increased and fecundity decreased as dosage increased (Table II). Reproduction was strongly inhibited at 15 mg and completely inhibited at 18 mg. However, such inhibited nematodes rapidly resumed both growth and reproduction within 2 days after transfer to a Procaine-free medium, but (as shown in Table II) these nematodes were smaller and had fewer offspring than the untreated animals.

TABLE II

Effects of Procaine on growth and reproduction of
Caenorhabditis briggsae and reversal when nematodes
were transferred to drug-free medium. [1]

Treatment	Body length(μ) day 5	Body length(μ) day 7	Offspring/ Adult
Untreated	863	1121	104
Procaine- 9 mg/ml medium	473 **	601 **	46 **
Procaine-15 mg/ml medium	410 **	457 **	0.2**
Procaine-15 mg/ml medium reversed[2]		913 **	87 *
Procaine-18 mg/ml medium	365 **	369 **	0.0**
Procaine-18 mb/ml medium reversed[2]		902 **	80 *

[1]Each figure represents an average from 10 individually
cultured nematodes.
[2]Procaine treated nematodes transferred at day 5 to the
same medium without the drug.
*Significantly different from the control $p < 0.05$
**Significantly different from the control $p < 0.01$

By transferring the nematodes to medium without
Procaine following exposure to an inhibitory dosage for
varying time periods, it was shown that even beyond day 14,
when reproduction normally ceases, inhibited nematodes can
still reproduce (Table III). Thus, Procaine can alter the
reproduction cycle so that the reproductive periods of
treated and untreated nematodes would not coincide at any
time. In this experiment, significant increases in
longevity occurred for several exposure levels of longer
than 10 days, but this effect was not consistent.

Nematodes exposed to 9 mg showed significantly less
osmotic fragility and a lower specific gravity at 3 weeks
than did untreated nematodes of the same age (Table IV).
Thus, with respect to these two parameters which characterize aging in C. briggsae, Procaine-treated nematodes
appeared to be biologically young even though they were
chronologically old.

TABLE III

The effects on reproduction and longevity of
Caenorhabditis briggsae after transfer to drug-
free medium following different time intervals
of exposure to 15 mg Procaine/ml medium.[1]

Transfer (day)[2]	Reproduction		Longevity- 50% alive (day)
	Start (day)	Duration (days)	
Not trans-ferred	-	-	30
1	4.5	9.5	29
2	5	10	28
3	6	10	28
4	7	8	28
5	7	8	32
6	9	8	30
7	10	11	32
8	10	8	31
9	10	8	31
10	11	6	32
11	13	7	33 *
12	14	7	34 *
13	15	7	33
14	16	7	34 *
17	18	5	33
18	19	6	32
19	21	5	32 *
20	22	4	32 *
21	23	2	32
Untreated	4.5	9.5	28

[1]Figures represent observations of 10 nematodes
at each level.
[2]Day after hatch that the nematodes were transferred to medium without Procaine.
*Significant differences from the untreated;
$p < 0.05$.

TABLE IV

Effects of Procaine on the osmotic fragility
and the specific gravity of 21 day-old
Caenorhabditis briggsae.

Treatment	Osmotic fragility[1] (%)	Specific gravity
Untreated	60	1.128
9 mg Procaine/ ml medium	20 *	1.104 *

[1]Based on the number of nematodes which
burst after 15 min in distilled water.
*p $<$ 0.01

DISCUSSION

The mechanisms involved in the delay in the development of increased specific gravity and osmotic fragility
in C. briggsae are not known, but the similarity of these
changes for both human erythrocytes and nematodes suggests
a possible pathway. Prankerd (1958) believes that changes
with age in the osmotic fragility and specific gravity of
human red blood cells are related to corresponding changes
in membrane permeability and energy potential within such
cells. With age, the erythrocytes tend to lose their
lipid contents (mostly phospholipids) by peroxidation,
thus affecting their energy potentials which are necessary
for maintaining normal cationic concentration gradients.
Prankerd postulated that this lipid loss accounts for the
increased specific gravity. Lipid peroxidation and the
attendant age-related accumulation of lipofuscin has been
demonstrated for two free-living nematodes, including
C. briggsae (Buecher and Hansen, 1973; Epstein et al.,
1972). It is possible that similar pathways for these
age-related changes exist between red blood cells and
nematodes.

It is also appropriate to speculate on the
possible mechanisms involved in the effects on growth and
reproduction of C. briggsae. Procaine is known to block

conduction of nerve impulses (Bucci and Saunders, 1960),
an action which is both dependent on the concentration of
the anaesthetic and is also reversible. This action is
thought to be due to the drug being a reversible monoamine
oxidase inhibitor (MacFarlane, 1973; Hrachovec, 1973),
which causes alterations in the metabolism of monoamines
such as serotonin and catecholamine, compounds which act
as neurohumoral transmittors in the central nervous system.
Serotonin was recently demonstrated in nematodes by Anya
(1973). The link between the present nematode investigation and those studies of the actions of Procaine on
mammalian nerve tissues was provided by microlaser beam
investigations which indicated that nematode growth and
gonad development are mediated by nervous control (Samoiloff, 1973). Samoiloff's studies showed that destruction
of the nematode nerve ring by laser beam microsurgery
resulted in the inhibition of gonad growth. The rapid
resumption of growth and the start of reproduction a short
time after termination of exposure to Procaine in the
current studies demonstrated the reversibility of effects
of the drug on the nervous system and also provides additional evidence of nervous control of gonad development.

We are currently evaluating the effects of Procaine
on other parameters which characterize senescence in C.
briggsae, such as the age-related decrease in net negative
membrane surface charge and the increase in age pigment
content with age.

REFERENCES

Anya, A.O. (1973). Comp. Gen. Pharmacol. 4, 149.
Bjorksten, J. (1971). Finska Kemistsamfundets Medd. 80, 23.
Bucci, L. and Saunders, J.C. (1960). J. Neuropsychiat. 1,
    276.
Buecher, E. and Hansen, E.L. (1973). 2nd Intern. Congr.
    Plant Pathol. abstr. 210.
Danon, D., Goldstein, L., Marikovsky, Y. and Skutelsky, E.
    (1972). J. Ultrastruct. Res. 38, 500.
Danon, D. and Marikovsky, Y. (1964). J. Lab. Clin. Med. 64,
    668.
Epstein, J., Himmelhoch, S. and Gershon, D. (1972).
    Mechanisms of Ageing and Development 1, 245.
Gershon, H. and Gershon, D. (1970). Nature, (London) 227,
    1214.

Hrachovec, J.P. (1973). The Gerontologist 13, 62.

Kisiel, M., Himmelhoch, S. and Zuckerman, B.M. (1974). Exp. Parasitol. (in press).

Kisiel, M., Nelson, B. and Zuckerman, B.M. (1972). Nematologica 18, 373.

Kohn, R. (1971). "Principles of Mammalian Aging." Prentice-Hall Inc., Englewood Cliffs, N.J.

Krusberg, L.R. (1971). In "Plant Parasitic Nematodes", Vol. 2 (B.M. Zuckerman, W.F. Mai and R.A. Rohde, eds.), pp. 213-234, Academic Press, New York.

MacFarlane, M.D. (1973). J. Am. Geriat. Soc. 21, 414.

Prankerd, T.A.J. (1958). J. Physiol. (London) 143, 325.

Samoiloff, M.R. (1973). Science 180, 976.

Sayre, F.W., Hansen, E.L. and Yarwood, E.A. (1963). Exp. Parasitol. 13, 98.

Zeelon, P., Gershon, H. and Gershon, D. (1973). Biochemistry 12, 1743.

Zuckerman, B.M., Himmelhoch, S. and Kisiel, M. (1973). Nematologica 19, 109.

Zuckerman, B.M., Himmelhoch, S., Nelson, B., Epstein, J. and Kisiel, M. (1971). Nematologica 17, 478.

Zuckerman, B.M., Nelson, B. and Kisiel, M. (1972). J. Nematol. 4, 261.

DISCUSSION SUMMARY

Ruth B. Weg, Ph.D.

University of Southern California
Ethel Percy Andrus Gerontology Center
Los Angeles, California

Although it is a long time (Second and Third Centuries, B.C.) since the Taoist philosophy and elaborate practices for achieving long life and preservation of its essence (semen), the study of aging is, in some respects, still in a 'prescriptive' stage.

At this symposium, as with a number of recent conferences on aging, there was widespread agreement as to the apparent complexity of the processes of aging. Equally impressive has been the lack of agreement of cause and effect in the exploration of theories of aging. The last ten years have been characterized by data in support of one or another molecular theory of aging. Nevertheless, it remains very difficult to organize the findings resulting from varied research designs with different living systems into a testable perspective.

It is prudent, however, to utilize what information from each (i.e., the programmed theory of aging, the mutation theory, the autoimmune theory, the crosslinkage theory, the free radical theory, and the genetic and non-genetic theories) can fit into a structure that may realize the most reasonable, coherent interpretation of diverse data, increase the capacity for predictions, and provide insight into the cause-and-effect relationships of the multidimensional changes known as 'aging'. The proliferation of theories and of some data has mitigated against the identification of any one critical reaction or any one constituent of living systems as the primary fact of aging. Continued investigation of molecular changes accompanying increasing age has multiplied the mass of unrelated information. Reintegration of such data into the functioning organism is therefore necessary before any theoretical

187

mechanism(s) of aging are finally demonstrated to be coincident with the origin and reality of aging in the organism. There would appear to be an inevitability that ongoing research in pursuit of any one of the theories examined down to the molecular level would illuminate a critical if not primary role for the changing expression of the genome: programmed or stochastic, accurate or in error; throughout the life span -- i.e., in early differentiation, in development, in adulthood, and in senescence. The loss of genetic information or altered information in replication and/or transcription and/or translation would appear to be basic. That there must be a genetic base for longevity or life span is inescapable -- witness Leonard Hayflick's significant work with human cell cultures (1965), the species specific life span of most living systems (Rockstein, 1966, 1972; Comfort, 1964), and the data from studies of monozygotic and dizygotic twins (Kallman and Jarvik, 1959). It is also inescapable that studies which use life span as the measuring stick reveal little about mechanisms of aging, or the rate of aging.

It may even be as Alex Comfort (1971) has suggested that "luckily we don't have to find out which of these mechanisms is instrumental in aging. We can alter its rate without knowing." He is confident that techniques for the slowing and reversing of aging may be close at hand (1972). However, pharmacological studies related to the alteration of life span of cells, and experimental animals -- including the effects of antioxidants, radioprotectors, amino suppressive chemicals, hormones, lathyrogens and sulfonamides -- are suggestive, yet often equivocal (Bellamy, 1968; Bender,1965; Bender et al.,1970; Harman, 1968; Kormendy and Bender, 1971a, b; La Bella, 1966; Nandy and Bourne, 1966). Clinical studies of treatment and drug therapies to retard or alleviate symptoms accompanying aging have been equally suggestive and equally equivocal (Aslan, 1972; Berryman et al., 1961; Goldfarb et al., 1972; MacFarlane, 1973).

Theories tested and found inadequate or incomplete in the research laboratories and in the larger laboratory of world activities continue to receive attention; e.g., the somatic mutation theory. The somatic mutation theory, as such, was in earlier days supported by radiation studies of Curtis et al. (1964) and Curtis (1968). However, the survivors of the atomic disaster of Nagasaki and Hiroshima

(Hollingsworth et al., 1962), exposed and nonexposed groups matched for age and sex, provide very significant data, i.e., no differences were found in age-related physiological deterioration -- determined by periodic measurement of systolic and diastolic blood pressure, vital capacity, heart size, hearing acuity, skin elasticity, progressive hair greying and a variety of immunologic tests. Radiation which increased the incidence of cancer and brought about premature death, was unrelated to the acceleration of aging and, therefore, not a reasonable model of aging. Since radiation is a potent mutagen, yet failed to increase the rate of aging, the usefulness of the somatic mutation theory for aging is questionable. A further question may be raised from the work with radiomimetic substances which do not shorten the life span and do not result in speeding up of age-related pathology (Alexander, 1967).

One area not touched on may prove to be the very critical one -- particularly in relation to human aging. The unique quality of being human is inexorably tied to the development of the central nervous system. There is a reasonable argument presented by George Sacher in which he calls for study of systems and the complete living organism. Since the doubling of the human life span within the past two million years is surely related to brain development, the investigation of the coordinating neuroendocrine systems in development and aging is of major importance -- but not on a molecular, in vitro level alone (Sacher, 1968).

If one of the most characteristic changes with time is the decreasing capacity for homeostatic maintenance, then those data and theories which try to dissect the mechanisms of homeostasis need more attention. Sites of homeostatic control in the neuroendocrine system (such as the hypothalamus) are clearly implicated in changes through the life span. In the experiments of Clemens et al.(1969) reactivation of ovarian cycles in post oestrus female rats (23 months) was achieved by electrical stimulation of the preoptic area of the hypothalamus. This is persuasive evidence that the functional aging of the ovary may be determined not by the ovary alone but by some age-related change in an integrating central nervous system tissue -- in this instance, the hypothalamus. In another example, it has been demonstrated that aging effects may be found not only in a particular tissue or cell, but in an

integrating, stimulating part of the central nervous
system which coordinates the hormonal interactions in the
organism. Livers of old mice have a decreased ability to
synthesize the enzyme tyrosine aminotransferase. Upon
injection of hormones known to act on liver, the enzyme
was induced with the same kinetics in old as for the young
mice; the old liver cells had greater potential for response than earlier evidenced (Finch, 1973). The delay
was elsewhere -- either in stimulation from the CNS or the
decreased responsivity of the glands to the neuronal stimulus.

At the Presidential Symposium of the Gerontological
Society (Miami, Florida, November, 1973), Dr. David Danon
of Israel talked of the relatively unchanged condition of
the aged since Biblical days. He invoked the 'era of
research on the membrane' as significant for understanding
the genesis of aging. It is indeed conceivable that some
of the changes with time (in the speed and responsivity of
neuronal, endocrine, and immune systems), may relate to
membrane alterations, which in turn may relate to genic
modifications. Perhaps one of the most important contributions in the past fifteen years to the study of aging and
the re-evaluation of existing knowledge and theories is
the significant work of one of the principal participants
in this two-day symposium, microbiologist Leonard Hayflick
(1965, 1970). The techniques of human diploid cell culture
have identified what is no doubt the potential life span
of most human cells, with the exception of germ cells. The
immortality of human cells as a 'given', suggested by the
early experiments of Alexis Carrel, must now be discarded.
Immortality, as a goal of intervention, may nevertheless
remain the dream of many. Further, the successful enuclea-
tion of such cells (Wright and Hayflick, 1972, 1973) and
continued culture of cytoplasms and nuclei makes possible
a more careful examination of the role of each and consti-
tuents thereof in phase three (degeneration/death) changes.
Chimeras of young and old cytoplasms and nuclei will also
enlarge our knowledge of possible mechanisms of aging
pacemakers, in the nucleus, cytoplasm and/or membrane.

In the end, there is the plague of fragmentation in
the study of gerontology and in its theorizing. However,
this symposium provided a most valuable opportunity to
overview the state of the art. New technology, more
molecular data, and even new theories will not compute

(individually or together) the answer to the mechanism(s) of aging. Greater focus on testable mechanisms of aging in the physiology of the whole organism is needed. Significant differences between young and old are at the level of interacting systems, not at rest but in action to maintain homeostasis in face of the countless daily changes in the internal and external environments. The data on the decrease in homeostatic balance with age, suggestive data from stimulation of the hypothalamic area of old animals, and the knowledge that human cells in culture have a limited life span correlated with the age of the donor hold promise for the next symposium on human aging. I join with Dr. Nathan Shock in his eloquent plea at the meeting for not another new theory but a continual reintegration of the accumulating data into the total functional organism.

REFERENCES

Alexander, P. (1967). In "Aspects of the Biology of Ageing" (Symposium of the Society for Experimental Biology, No. 21) (H. W. Woolhouse, ed.), pp. 29-50, Academic Press, New York.

Aslan, A. (1972). Proc. 9th Intern. Congr. Gerontol. Symposia Reports 2, 115.

Bellamy, D. (1968). Exp. Gerontol. 3, 327.

Bender, A. D. (1965). Exp. Gerontol. 1, 237.

Bender, A. D., Kormendy, C. G. and Powell, R. (1970). Exp. Gerontol. 5, 97.

Berryman, J. A. W., Forbes, H. A. W. and Simpson-White, R. (1961). Brit. Med. J. 5268, 1683.

Clemens, J. A., Amenamori, Y., Jenkins, T. and Meites, J. (1969). Soc. Exp. Biol. Med. 132, 561.

Comfort, A. (1964). "Aging: The Biology of Senescence." Holt, Rinehart and Winston, New York.

Comfort, A. (1971). Playboy, pp. 114, 209.

Comfort, A. (1972). 25th Annual Meeting Gerontol. Soc., San Juan, Puerto Rico, December 1972.

Curtis, H. J. (1968). In "The Biological Basis of Medicine" (E. Bittar and N. Bittar, eds.), Vol. 1, Academic Press, New York.

Curtis, H. J., Telley, J. and Crowley, C. (1964). Radiation Res. 22, 730.

Finch, C. E. (1973). In "Development and Aging of the

Nervous System" (M. Rockstein and M. L. Sussman, eds.),
pp. 199-213, Academic Press, New York.

Goldfarb, A., Hochstadt, N., Jacobson, J. and Weinstein,
E. A. (1972). J. Gerontol. 27, 212.

Harman, D. (1968). J. Gerontol. 23, 276.

Hayflick, L. (1965). Exp. Cell Res. 37, 614.

Hayflick, L. (1970). Exp. Gerontol. 5, 291.

Hollingsworth, J. W., Bebe, G. W., Ishida, M. and Brill, A.
B. (1962). In "The Uses of Vital and Health Statistics
for Genetic and Radiation Studies", Atomic Bomb Casualty
Commission, Hiroshima and Nagasaki, pp. 77-100, United
Nations, New York.

Kallman, F. J. and Jarvik, L. F. (1959). In "Handbook of
Aging and the Individual" (J. E. Birren, ed.), pp. 216-
263, University of Chicago Press, Chicago.

Kormendy, C. G. and Bender, A. D. (1971a). Gerontologia 17,
52.

Kormendy, C. G. and Bender, A. D. (1971b). J. Pharm. Sci.
60, 167.

La Bella, F. S. (1966). The Gerontologist 6, 46.

MacFarlane, M. D. (1973). J. Am. Geriat. Soc. 21, 414.

Nandy, K. and Bourne, G. H. (1966). Nature 210, 313.

Rockstein, M. (1966). In "Topics in the Biology of Aging"
(P. O. Krohn, ed.), pp. 43-61, Interscience Publica-
tions, New York.

Rockstein, M. (1972). In "Molecular Genetic Mechanisms of
Development and Aging" (M. Rockstein and G. T. Baker,
III, eds.), pp. 1-10, Academic Press, New York.

Sacher, G. A. (1968). Exp. Gerontol. 3, 265.

Wright, W. E. and Hayflick, L. (1972). Exp. Cell Res. 74,
187.

Wright, W. E. and Hayflick, L. (1973). Proc. Soc. Exp.
Biol. Med. 144, 587.

A 4
B 5
C 6
D 7
E 8
F 9
G 0
H 1
I 2
J 3